THE SHADOWS

AT POLYDOR

MALCOLM CAMPBELL

IDMON PUBLICATIONS

PEGSWOOD, MORPETH 2003

Published by
Malcolm Campbell
(Idmon Publications)
PO Box 160
MORPETH
Northumberland NE61 6WY
England UK
E-mail: shads@malcolmcampbell.me.uk
Website: http://www.malcolmcampbell.me.uk

First published 2003

Typeset by Malcolm Campbell
Printed and bound by:
SHAW Printing
Pegswood, Morpeth

Title Page The three core members of the band at Leeds Grand Theatre in 1986, photographed by John Humphrey

A CIP catalogue record for this book is available from the British Library

ISBN 0 9535567 2 7

CONTENTS

INTRODUCTION

ANNUAL SURVEYS, 1980-PRESENT

PREFACE AND ACKNOWLEDGEMENTS

This book looks in detail at The Shadows' recorded output, and the various releases stemming from it, since their move to Polydor in 1980, so picking up where *The Shadows At EMI* left off.

A significant proportion of this output was made up of instrumental renditions of vocal hit Singles of the 1980s, which, while appealing to the general public who put successive Albums into the charts, have generally met with a cool reception from the more confined circle of their long-term fans. In the main, the former category of record buyer would not have started off with preconceived notions of what The Shadows should sound like, or what kind of material The Shadows should be concerning themselves with, and I have endeavoured to do the same in evaluating the cover versions. In considering them in relation to the originals, I have come to the not unsurprising conclusion that some covers are better than others, and to the further conclusion, which some may not welcome, that there are several covers which are easily the equal of the group compositions of the period, and some which are arguably even better. In any event, they all deserve to be viewed individually against the musical tastes (and, just as importantly, the recording techniques) of their particular decade. I do not expect anybody necessarily to agree with my findings, but I hope that they will encourage debate, which so far has been signally lacking, with whole Albums sometimes dismissed indiscriminately without discussion.

On this occasion I have not included a formal Bibliography, since most of the literature on The Shadows focuses primarily on the 1960s and, to a lesser degree, the 1970s. I have naturally looked for guidance (though I do not invariably follow them) to a number of the authorities mentioned in the previous two books, notably the Discographies of **Bernard Broche, Pierre Cortada, Otto Kasper** and **Detlev Sackenheim**, together with the exemplary Websites of **John Panteny** (who kindly provided scans for some overseas releases), **John Campbell, David Dixon, David Martin** and **Leo's Den Direct**.

George Geddes' ground-breaking *The Shadows: A History And Discography* stopped short at the early 1980s, which was bad news for me in putting this book together and is bad news for Shadows fans everywhere; his knowledge of Shadows-inspired music, concert performances and so on is immense, and it is to be hoped that in due course an updated edition will see the light of day.

My greatest debt in the sphere of the written word is to the many acute and sensitive observations on Shadstrax of the period by **Rob Bradford** (in *Record Collector*, fanzines and disc annotations): I could not begin to match what he has to say, so I have quoted from him frequently. I have taken issue with him on one major point (see the Introduction under "The Shadows Uncovered"): the reason he figures so prominently in the discussion is not the result of any animosity (I think Rob would agree with me that we are on the best of terms!), but simply because he is by far the most eloquent and challenging advocate of his particular viewpoint.

This time round I can thank two distinguished photographers for placing at my disposal some of their fine work. **John Hank Humphrey** actually wrote to me unasked with an offer of help in June 1998, before my first Shadows book appeared, but I was not then at the stage of grappling with pictures as well as text! I had the good fortune to come across John this year at Reading and again at York, and what you see in this book is the result of our deliberations. At Reading too John introduced me to **David Hawley**, who also generously offered to contribute and came up with a most impressive set of pics. Further discussions with both at Shadowmania 2002 helped to clarify several points, and I am grateful to them for taking the time to deal with my queries.

It is a pleasure to thank a number of other individuals who have given me assistance: **Tony Hoffman**, editor of *Shadsfax*, continues to keep fans fully informed of all that is important in Shadows' circles; **Bernie O'Hara** kindly made available to me unpublished Top Twenty Placings for certain categories of the *Shadsfax Poll 2001* which he organised; **Ulrich Sasu**, author of the database *The Shadows File*, provided much invaluable discographical information; **Jim Nugent** helped out with cover versions; warm thanks also to **Brian Berg, Victor Dubiler, Brian Goode, Allister Hardwick, Peter Lewry, Ray Liffen and Alan Taylor** (*Pipeline* it goes without saying has proved a priceless resource)**, Peter Monk, Ed Montano**, **Ray Steer**, **George White** (check out his truly excellent book on UK EPs, ISBN 0 9519888 1 6), **Gabriel Zeldin**; also to **Carly** from Music Zone's Mail Order Department at Stockport for being so patient and helpful.

A special mention for **Pat and John Read** of Leo's Den Music Direct, who have kept me informed about the latest releases and often taken the trouble to reply in great detail to my questions — fans of Cliff & The Shadows are indeed fortunate in having this invaluable resource at their disposal. I am most grateful too for all the friendly and patient help and advice given me by **Allan Lynn, Darren Turner and Bruce Weightman** at SHAW Printing, Pegswood.

This time I have also benefited directly from an expert eye, and the present book is most certainly the better for it: **Les Woosey**, who, I am delighted to say, has agreed to join forces with me in producing (in 2003, we hope) an updated, enlarged and illustrated edition of the CD *Guide*, generously offered to look over the typescript. He came back in record time with many searching comments on details and caused me to think again about much that I had written; it is only fair to add that any errors or misjudgements are to be attributed to me.

Once again I am grateful to **Dorothy, Michael and Richard** for support and practical assistance. My two sons (**Michael** ably aided by **Tracy**) never ceased to amaze me with the ingenious way they dealt with the various picture covers and other illustrative material, and they were constantly on hand for informed advice on the actual music; they also played no small part in easing a former Apple Mac user's conversion to the wonderful but sometimes perplexing world of the PC, scanners and the rest. On a more general level, I have to say that my interest in music has never been confined to The Shadows (or their golden period) by any means, and through the influence and expertise of both Michael and Richard I have come to know and admire a wealth of music of various genres from the 1980s, 1990s and into this new century. Ian MacDonald no doubt has his adherents when he philosophizes in his illuminating study of The Beatles about "the catastrophic decline of pop" since the 1960s, but I am not one of them.

Pegswood, Morpeth: January 2003 MC

The author would be pleased to hear of any matters arising from this book: he can be contacted at

shads@malcolmcampbell.me.uk

Further information on this and other Shadows books, including the projected update of the *CD Guide*, can be found at his Website

http://www.malcolmcampbell.me.uk

The frontmen in action, Nottingham 1990
Photograph: John Hank Humphrey

And again at Bornemouth, 29 November 1990
Photograph: David Hawley

Brian Bennett at Nottingham, 1990
Photograph: John Hank Humphrey

INTRODUCTION: I

REVIEW OF VINYL AND CD RELEASES

A. SINGLES

1

On Polydor UK The Shadows released 7" Singles from August 1980 through to December 1989 (with a re-release of the last in September 1990): seventeen[1] in all, of which only the first (#1[2]) and the third (#6) charted, at No. 50 and No. 44 respectively. None appeared in 1985 or 1988; there were two in 1980, three in 1981, two in 1982, two in 1983, one in 1984, three in 1986, two in 1987, two in 1989.

There was also a separate special edit of an A-side in December 1983 (GOING HOME, see #22); and a purely Promo Single taking in two Album tracks in July 1989 (#54). A solitary 12" Single was put out in September 1986 (#38); and two CD Singles in 1989 (#50; and #55, identical in content to the 7").

2

The B-sides of the seventeen 7" Singles were without exception composed by Marvin Welch and Bennett. Only three of the A-sides had a group-connection: #43 PULASKI and #49 MOUNTAINS OF THE MOON, both the work of Bennett; and #55 (partial), the medley SHADOWMIX.

It is noteworthy that the originals of the borrowed A-sides were predominantly either instrumentals (i) or instrumentals existing beside vocal versions (ii), thus:
(i) EQUINOXE (PART V), MOZART FORTE, THE THIRD MAN, TELSTAR, THEME FROM MISSING, DIAMONDS, GOING HOME
(ii) THEMES FROM EASTENDERS & HOWARDS' WAY, WALKING IN THE AIR

---

[1] The two most widely distributed overseas were THE THIRD MAN (#6) and THEME FROM MISSING (#13); seven were confined to the UK.
[2] Items prefaced with symbol # refer to the releases documented in the Annual Surveys making up the bulk of this book.

The exceptions: IMAGINE: WOMAN, MOONLIGHT SHADOW, DANCING IN THE DARK; and the only two Shadows' vocals among the seventeen, TREAT ME NICE and (a Shadows' "exclusive") ON A NIGHT LIKE THIS.

3

The material for UK Singles could also be found on LP, with the following exceptions:

A-sides		
#1	1980	EQUINOXE (PART V) (edit)
#37	1986	DANCING IN THE DARK (7" remix)
Also (DJ edit version):		
#22	1983	GOING HOME
B-sides		
#1	1980	FENDER BENDER
#6	1981	THE FOURTH MAN
#12	1982	SPOT THE BALL
#13	1982	THE SHADY LADY
#18	1983	ELEVENIS
On 12" Single		
#38	1986	DANCING IN THE DARK (12" remix)

Thus the only A/B Single not found on LP is the 1980 EQUINOXE (PART V) (edit) / FENDER BENDER.

4

These are the particular Albums from which the UK Singles tracks were derived:

• *Change Of Address* (1980)

#3	1980	MOZART FORTE / MIDNIGHT CREEPIN'
#43	1987	— / CHANGE OF ADDRESS
#45	1987	— / OUTDIGO
#55	1989	— / ARTY'S PARTY

• *Hits Right Up Your Street* (1981)

#6	1981	THE THIRD MAN / —
#7	1981	TELSTAR / SUMMER LOVE '59
#9	1981	IMAGINE: WOMAN / HATS OFF TO WALLY
#24	1984	— / THING-ME-JIG

• *Life In The Jungle* (1982)

#12	1982	TREAT ME NICE / —
#13	1982	THEME FROM MISSING / —
#22	1983	— / CAT 'N' MOUSE
#39	1986	— / NO DANCING!

• *The Silver Album / XXV* (1983)

#18	1983	DIAMONDS / —
#22	1983	GOING HOME / —

• *Guardian Angel* (1984)

#24	1984	ON A NIGHT LIKE THIS / —
#35	1986	— / JOHNNY STACCATO
#37	1986	— / TURNING POINT

• *Moonlight Shadows* (1986)

#35	1986	MOONLIGHT SHADOW / —

• *Simply ... Shadows* (1987)

#39	1986	THEMES FROM EASTENDERS ... / —
#43	1987	PULASKI / —
#45	1987	WALKING IN THE AIR / —

• *Steppin' To The Shadows* (1989)

#49	1989	MOUNTAINS OF THE MOON / STACK-IT

• *Reflection* (1990)

#55	1989	SHADOWMIX / —

— Also:

12" Single

• *Moonlight Shadows* (1986) ~ • *Guardian Angel* (1984)

#38	1986	— / DANCING IN THE DARK / TURNING POINT

CD Single

• *Change Of Address* (1980)

#55	1989	— / ARTY'S PARTY

• *Guardian Angel* (1984)

#50	1989	— / — / TURNING POINT

• *Steppin' To The Shadows* (1989)

#50	1989	MOUNTAINS OF THE MOON / STACK-IT / —

• *Reflection* (1990)

#55	1989	SHADOWMIX / —

Hence the same Album provided both A- and B-sides in only four cases: #3, 7, 9, 49.

5

Overseas Singles. Aside from a solitary French Promo sourced from *Guardian Angel* (#28), there are a mere eight exclusively overseas Singles pairings: see #4 (Belgium/ Holland: *not* Germany, as often stated!), #5 (Bolivia), #10 (Italy), #11 (Holland), #16 (Finland), #31 and #46 (New Zealand), #32 (Australia).

Tracks that do not figure on UK Singles:
INDIGO / — (#4), — / TEMPTATION (#5), — / ALBATROSS (#10), CHI MAI / — (#11), CHARIOTS OF FIRE / LIFE IN THE JUNGLE (#16), HOW DO I LOVE THEE / — (#31), HAMMERHEAD / CAN'T PLAY YOUR GAME (#32).

B. ALBUMS

I: UK ALBUMS

1

Primary Albums (1980–1990). Releases and re-releases: of the twelve Albums in question, the first six were initially issued on vinyl LP. Column 1 below gives LP title, column 2 the year of LP release and where apposite re-release, column 3 the year of CD release and where apposite re-release.

Change Of Address	1980/ 1983	1992
Hits Right Up Your Street	1981/ 1984	1987/ 1992
Life In The Jungle	1982/ 1985	1989/ 1992
Live At Abbey Road	1982	1989/ 2001
The Silver Album [2LP]	1983	None
XXV	1983	1987

The practice of following up an LP release with a budget issue three years further on was dropped after *Life In The Jungle*: *Live At Abbey Road* was anyway a UK giveaway with *Life In The Jungle*, and *The Silver Album* was a one-off mail order project, while *XXV*, though it made the Top Forty, was never taken wholly seriously by fans or critics, duplicating as it did so much of the new material on *The Silver Album*. In any case, by 1986[3] or so vinyl sales were in steady decline, and the eventual market domination of Compact Disc could be taken as an absolute certainty (whatever vinyl devotees were asserting to the contrary). In fact, two of the six Albums were put out on CD in 1987, and four of the six were digitised before the 80s had passed.

The final six Albums were issued in both LP and CD format concurrently. Column 1 below gives Album title, column 2 date of first issue, column 3 date of CD re-release[4] where apposite.

Guardian Angel	1984	1998 [augmented]
Moonlight Shadows	1986	1996
Simply ... Shadows	1987	1999
Steppin' To The Shadows	1989	1993
The Shadows At Their Very Best	1989	None
Reflection	1990	None

CDs come and CDs go as record companies think fit, so inevitably the entire back catalogue is unlikely to be available at any given point in time. Much has been done recently to fill gaps. Urgent desiderata at the time of writing are remastered CDs of *Change Of Address* and *Life In The Jungle*, preferably with detailed sleeve-notes; and among the very latest deletions announced for 2002, the most significant for our purposes is *Reflection*.[5]

---

3 Notwithstanding, 1986 saw the appearance of the "sampler" *The Shadows Showcase* (#40) from Reader's Digest, in LP/ cassette format only — though it has to be remembered that concerns such as this were catering for a relatively conservative audience, a significant proportion of whom would not even be contemplating at this stage a switch to a wholly new medium.

4 "Re-releases" on the same label possessing only minor cosmetic changes are disregarded here.

5 Perhaps on one or other of these candidates for reissue the 7" version of DANCING IN THE DARK (still a stranger to CD, see on #91!) could be incorporated.

2

Primary Album released after 1990: *The Shadows Live At The Liverpool Empire*; from See For Miles in 2001 as part of a 2CD set, first legitimate release, see on #93 in the main text.

3

Compilation Albums to 1990:
Polydor made an early concession to the Compact Disc format by releasing *Compact Shadows* in 1984 (see on #26 for the range of tracks provided). Otherwise[6], it was left to Pickwick to pick up some hitherto undigitised material in a set of three discs, whose content turned out to be far superior to their physical composition (see on #62, *A Special Collection*).

So, by 1990, the year of *Reflection*, Polydor had put out ten Shadows' Albums on CD, plus one compilation; licensee Pickwick had issued three compilation-Albums. By this same year EMI UK (after a slow start) and licensees likewise had made fourteen issues available[7] — drawing of course on a much more extensive catalogue.

4

Compilation Albums, 1991 to present.

The years 1991/92 mark the final demise of the LP as a medium for Shadows' Polydor material[8], as for much else: in 1991 Polydor issued *Themes And Dreams* in both LP and CD format, while Reader's Digest marketed its mammoth *The Shadows Collection* as an 8LP or 6CD set; in 1992 Polydor/ Polytel offered *The Shadows: Complete* as either 3LP or 3CD.

---

6 There was also the hybrid (EMI + Polydor tracks) "sampler", *Relaxing With The Shadows*, from Reader's Digest (1990, see #61).

7 Disappointingly, all save four were compilations. Even more disappointingly, EMI only stirred itself to issue one primary Album (*String Of Hits*, a vinyl best-seller of course), the other three being farmed out (see *CD Guide* 40, under "1990").

8 The writing was already on the wall with the release by Pickwick of *The Shadows Collection* and *Diamonds* on LP and CD (1989/90), but *Dancing In The Dark* on CD only (1991; 1990 in CD Box Set).

Categories of music recorded by The Shadows during their association with Polydor are discussed in some detail in the next section of this Introduction. Examined here in broad terms is the content of each and every Album issued between 1991 and the present. Compilations were made up of:

A/1

Chart-related cover versions exclusively (a very clear majority):

#65 *Themes And Dreams* Polydor 1991

#66 *The Shadows Collection* (EMI, + 45 Polydor tracks) Reader's Digest 1991

#71 *Shadows In The Night* Polydor 1993

#73 *Dreamtime* Spectrum 1993

#74 *The Shadows* PolyGram Special Products for Avon Cosmetics 1993

#88 *50 Golden Greats* (EMI, + 6 Polydor tracks) EMI 2000

A/2

"Self-covers", drawing on the remakes of the classic hits on *The Shadows At Their Very Best* (#56):

#92 *The Hit Sound Of The Shadows* (18 of the 20 tracks of *Very Best*, plus Polydor remake of RIDERS IN THE SKY; and "oldie" THE THIRD MAN) Universal/ Connoisseur 2001

A/3

Chart-related covers + "self-covers" + original group compositions:

#70 *The Shadows: Complete* [includes all 20 of *Very Best*] Polydor/ Polytel 1992

A/4

Original group-compositions exclusively:

#79 *Shadstrax* See For Miles 1998

There are also joint collections, made up of tracks by Hank Marvin and tracks by The Shadows. Categories of Shadows material therein:

B/1

Cover versions (x 6):

#78 *Hank Marvin And The Shadows Play The Music Of Andrew Lloyd Webber And Tim Rice*, PolyGram TV 1997

B/2

Cover versions (x 5) + "self-covers" (x 11):

#76 *The Best Of Hank Marvin And The Shadows* PolyGram TV 1994

Cover versions (x 6) + "self-covers" (x 20):

#80 *The Very Best Of Hank Marvin & The Shadows: The First 40 Years*, PolyGram TV 1998

B/3

Cover versions + group originals:

#91 *Hank Marvin & The Shadows: The Singles Collection* 2 issues, Music Club and Crimson, both 2001

II: OVERSEAS ALBUMS[9]

1

To 1990:

Nothing novel is on offer. Polydor material was strictly controlled, with no throwback to the earlier days of EMI, when weird and wonderful alternative versions could turn up, whether by accident or design, in overseas locations, and thence to record presses outwith the UK; or when personnel in EMI France, for example, could take it upon themselves to tamper in one way or another (but invariably for the worse) with the original sound-balance.

There were six compilations during this period, all but the last (CD/LP) in LP format:

#17	1982	*Space Hits*	Holland
#23	1983	*20 Golden Greats Vol. 2*	New Zealand
#33	1985	*More Rarities*	New Zealand
#34	1985	*Sounds Of Today* [2LP]	Australia
#47	1987	*The Shadows In The Eighties*	Australia
#48	1987	*Guitars In Love*	Holland

The 2LP *Sounds Of Today* scarcely counts: it is the UK *The Shadows Silver Album* (#19) with running-orders altered, see on #34. Of the rest, the three Australian issues blend EMI and Polydor material[10]; Polydor cover versions occupy two of these, but the *More Rarities* set has five group-composed B-sides, together with SHADOOGIE '83. The two Dutch Albums again offer covers in the main, raising only three group-originals between them.

---

[9] On the evidence of the data accumulated in this book, the three primary LPs most widely distributed overseas were *Change Of Address, Hits Right Up Your Street* and *Moonlight Shadows*; two were confined to the UK: *Live At Abbey Road* [given away free with *Life In The Jungle*], and *The Silver Album* [mail-order].

[10] For Shadows' product in relation to EMI Australia ~ Polydor Australia, see Ian Kershaw, *SCOFA* 30 (1992) 9.

2

1991 to present, all CD. There are not many:
Chart cover versions:
#83 *The Ballads* PolyGram South Africa 1998
Chart covers + "self-covers" + THE THIRD MAN:
#84 *Master Series: The Shadows* PolyGram TV Austria etc. 1998

EMI and Polydor tracks together[11]:
Chart covers:
#75 *The Shadows Collection* (CD2 = New Zealand LP #23, q.v.)
#87 *The Shadows Complete* Australia 1999, includes 18 Polydor tracks
#90 *Golden Greats* Japan 2000, 6 Polydor tracks as on UK *50 Golden Greats* above

Bristol 22 October 1990
Photograph: David Hawley

[11] Also #94 *Kon-Tiki* Norway 2001, but only a single Polydor track, EQUINOXE (PART V), edited version. See also under #95 (ALBATROSS).

Nottingham 1990
Photographs: John Hank Humphrey

INTRODUCTION: II

THE SHADOWS UNCOVERED

Over the Polydor years, fresh compositions by one or more group-members continued to appear, on both Singles and Albums. However, they were now very much in the minority: on some Albums there were barely any, or none at all, while the A-sides of all Singles prior to PULASKI in October 1987 were derivative.

In other words, The Shadows' Polydor output was largely based on the compositions of others, and by far the greater proportion of these was made up (almost uninterruptedly between 1986 and 1990) of numbers which had performed well (usually in the recent past[12]) in the popular music charts of the UK or USA or both. Such numbers came to be earmarked by means of Polydor-commissioned market research and submitted to the group for recording in a predominantly or exclusively "hits" package — first explicitly and comprehensively on the back cover of *Moonlight Shadows*: "Over 60 minutes of The Shadows' unique interpretations of classic tracks". It is this body of material that is generally referred to under the blanket term "cover versions".

There are of course further categories of "cover" material: so-called "standards" likely to have been familiar to most listeners (THE THIRD MAN is an example); or numbers which, though previously recorded, may not have been immediately familiar, if at all (as INDIGO or HELLO MR W.A.M. or BILITIS); or, stretching the definition somewhat, material which may not actually have been made public, but was submitted to the group in Demo form or came to their attention by some other route (as RIDERS OF THE RANGE or LIVERPOOL DAYS or GUARDIAN ANGEL).

---

[12] The 1989 RIGHT HERE WAITING, on the 1990 Album *Reflection*, can serve as an example of an up-to-date cover. But, as the tables below will make clear, covers can go much further back, taking in classic numbers such as the 1962 TELSTAR (on the 1981 *Hits Right Up Your Street*). Sometimes *remakes* of classic numbers will have played a part in track-selection, for instance behind SOMETHING'S GOTTEN HOLD OF MY HEART on *Reflection* lies the Marc Almond/ Gene Pitney chart-topper of 1989 rather than the Top Five Pitney version of 1967. Details of these will be found in the surveys presented in the main text.

Another broad class of "cover" can be distinguished, which, though stemming from an assortment of composers (including group-members), replicates numbers previously recorded by The Shadows themselves, i.e. "self-covers" such as SHADOOGIE ('83) on *The Shadows' Silver Album* of 1983.

The following two tables give a breakdown for nine Albums issued between 1980 and 1990. Three are excluded for present purposes: (i) *Live At Abbey Road*: not of course a typical Album, it was made up partly of previously released Polydor numbers; (ii) *The Silver Album*: this was a mixture of old and new material, but all save one (SHADOOGIE '83) of the fresh numbers turned up on *XXV*, which is used for the survey below; (iii) *The Shadows At Their Very Best*: an Album of "self-covers" (see above), which are only of incidental concern in what follows.

In the first table, column 1 gives Album title, column 2 total number of tracks on the Album, column 3 total of chart-related covers, column 4 total of other derivative tracks, column 5 group originals:

Change Of Address	12	6	2	4
Hits Right Up Your Street	16	11	1	4
Life In The Jungle	12	4	3	5
XXV	11	9	2	0
Guardian Angel	11	1	6	4
Moonlight Shadows	12[13]	12	0	0
Simply ... Shadows	16	14	1	1
Steppin' To The Shadows	16	12	1	3
Reflection	14 (+ 2)[14]	13	1	0
TOTALS	120 (+ 2)	82	17	21

13 Actually sixteen tracks: but four had been released on previous Albums.
14 These are the two "self-covers" not examined here: RIDERS IN THE SKY '90 (which could of course be construed as a "chart-cover"!) and the concoction SHADOWMIX.

In this second table the eighty two chart covers identified above are sorted by decade (but recent *remakes* take precedence over originals, see above):

		50s	*60s*	*70s*	*80s*
Change Of Address	6	0	2	4	0
Hits Right Up Your Street	11	0	2	3	6
Life In The Jungle	4	3	0	0	1
XXV	9	0	4	1	4
Guardian Angel	1	0	0	1	0
Moonlight Shadows	12	0	2	1	9
Simply ... Shadows	14	0	0	0	14
Steppin' To The Shadows	12	0	0	0	12
Reflection	13	0	0	0	13
TOTALS	82	3	10	10	59

The real "turning-point" in the approach to Album-making comes with the release of *Moonlight Shadows* in 1986: from then on the chart-related cover version from the 1980s is the single most important element in an Album's makeup — in fact the element chiefly responsible beyond any reasonable doubt for The Shadows' continued chart success; and maybe also for their continued functioning as a group.

****

Nobody with any interest in The Shadows' later recording career could be unaware of the volume of adverse criticism levelled at them for this heavy reliance on chart-orientated cover versions. Yet this contentious issue, with which successive interviewers in the 1990s have tenaciously confronted group members, has been given far more emphasis than it warrants. Everything I have read or heard suggests to me that Rob Bradford's judgement[15] is pretty representative of the general feeling.

He singles out as the prime offenders *Simply ... Shadows* and *Steppin' To The Shadows*, together with *Moonlight Shadows* (not quite as guilty). Consequently, this dense concentration of allegedly throwaway or dispensable tracks stems from a four-year span of the group's eleven year

15 In *Pipeline* 43 (1999) 38–39.

association with Polydor — and one of those four years was a sabbatical anyway! Put another way, if The Shadows had taken a more extended break and these three Albums had never seen the light of day, there would not have been, on any reasonable assessment, that much to argue (or complain) about.

Rob is more specific still: from this trio he would reckon with "thirty or so tracks" which "could be filed under 'Professional, skilful but ultimately forgettable'". The picture I paint of this Bottom Thirty is not quite so bleak, chiefly I suspect because I do not share Rob's loathing (his term) of what amounts to a pretty representative cross-section of mainstream 80's pop music[16] — any more than I share the opinion that the group originals are of a uniformly high standard. No, some are better than others, just as there are good 80s covers and bad 80s covers (or covers which are good in one respect but bad in another). At the very least, they deserve to be given a hearing, rather than to be consigned, collectively and unceremoniously, to the scrap-heap.

As indicated earlier, individual group members have been prompted by various interviewers to comment (invariably and inevitably in highly general terms) on the beleaguered "cover versions". The most notable I have come across are:

• Hank Marvin
Pipeline 20 (1993) 14; *Record Collector* No. 171 (November 1993) 97/ 99; *SCOFA* 35 (1996) 4; *Shadsfax* 25 [1999] 4
• Bruce Welch
SCOFA 31 (1993) 2 & 7
• Brian Bennett
Pipeline 25 (1994/95) 32–33
• Alan Jones
SCOFA 34 (1995) 4

[16] Six specimens of "contemporary chart slush" on *Moonlight*; almost all the eligible tracks on *Simply*, styled "contemporary chart fodder"; eleven on *Steppin'*, similarly judged. On this reckoning, the prospect of a "Stand Alone Factor" for any of these derivative numbers is ruled out before a note is played (or a synthesiser control activated).

There is little among the defensive responses that could — or indeed should — influence any evaluation of the covers, which have to be taken one by one on their merits. In the wise words of the historian A J P Taylor, "Men must be judged by what they do, not by what they say afterwards". But there is one point worth pursuing, adduced with evident approval by Rob Bradford in the article discussed above. This is an argument from arrangers Brian Bennett and Cliff Hall to the effect that, since they were pressed by Polydor to stick closely to the originals, "they might just as well have obtained the original backing tracks and simply replaced the vocals with Hank's lead guitar".[17]

We are dealing here not with a fact, but with a judgement, on a par with such comments as "It was really a demo album" (Brian Bennett of *Tasty*). It is one I view with some scepticism, given the repeated and emphatic insistence that a great deal of effort was put into the Albums in question.[18] And on this estimate what exactly are we to understand by the "special arrangements" attributed to Cliff Hall on record sleeves right up to 1990? In point of fact, there are plenty of counter examples to indicate that the group did *not* stick scrupulously to the originals, but did strive in various ways and to varying degrees to provide a distinctive product — to wit, 80s-Shadows instrumental interpretations of primarily high profile 80s-style vocal material.

More importantly, this apparently all-inclusive "might as well" argument undervalues what The Shadows did achieve in the Polydor years. To take a couple of examples from their very last Album, EYE OF THE TIGER and CROCKETT'S THEME easily equal and in some respects surpass their models in terms of sonority, atmosphere and sheer clout.

It can work both ways of course (this book does not set out to supply a totally clean bill of health by any means). ALWAYS ON MY MIND, for instance, is well served by the gloriously ringing lead guitar but let down very badly indeed by the pedestrian accompaniment, which sometimes resembles but does not begin to match the dazzling and adventurous version of The Pet Shop Boys (see on #59) .....

---

17 Compare Hank Marvin's remarks in the liner notes to the 1998 CD *Guardian Angel ... Plus*.

18 See in particular Brian Bennett in *Pipeline* 25 (1994/95) 36: "... we don't just knock the albums out. We spend a lot of time on them ..." and so on. In similar vein, and more tellingly still, the liner notes to the 1998 CD *Shadstrax*: "A lot of time, care, effort and *creativity* would go into arrangements ... You could still be *creative* within that framework" (italics mine).

The pivotal Shadows' Album of the 1980s was *Guardian Angel*. Here was a set with only one chart-related cover (and a pretty remote one at that); it sold abysmally by normal standards, in the region of 50,000 copies. "Thereafter it was back to recording albums of cover versions or risk losing their Polydor contract" (sleeve-notes to 1998 CD *Shadstrax*). I would not quarrel with this picture, except to say that it is only a partial picture, and not simply because the earlier *Change Of Address* and *Life In The Jungle*, which shifted significantly more copies, cannot reasonably be described as "cover Albums".

In fact, it is certain that the poor sales figures for *Guardian Angel* did not stem solely from its "purist" content. In the first place, as Jim Nugent has astutely pointed out[19], if the group had any enthusiasm for this Album, it did not make itself apparent in any of the numerous 1984 concert appearances. "Failure? I wonder how that happened?", as Jim puts it with his customary incisiveness.

A second contributory factor — and an even more telling one — is a point I have heard personally from so many that its validity can scarcely be doubted. Put quite simply, the group's fan-base of long standing began to contract markedly at around the time of *Life In The Jungle / XXV* or in some cases a bit later — not necessarily in the sense that people lost interest completely in The Shadows, but rather in the sense that, as one fan put it to me, they "suspended active interest in their current output": i.e., stopped buying their records!

One reason for this is that the group had long ceased to sound like a 60's band, and had already in the later part of the 70s, both in the studio and on stage, begun to reflect current trends by imbuing their music with denser textures and a synthesised backdrop.

It comes as no surprise then to find that in the 80s a significant proportion of their long-term supporters became increasingly disillusioned and even felt let down by their idols, who were felt somehow to have turned their backs on what was perceived as their "proper" sound — the vivid, sharply focused, atmospheric, less "processed" sound produced by the (seemingly) uncomplicated setup of guitars and drums: a million miles removed from the upstart synth-dominated productions of a brasher and more technologically orientated age.

[19] In *Pipeline* 44 (1999) 57.

Stylistically, *Guardian Angel* did go further along this path than previous Polydor Albums (though not that much further in a number of respects), and I myself knew committed Shadows' fans who at the time of its release would not give it the time of day. When Rob Bradford says (in the sleeve-notes referred to above) "Shadows' fans loved it", he seems to imply its immediate and enthusiastic acceptance, which is I believe (and as the sales figures confirm) quite mistaken. Indeed, here is what Rob himself had to say about *Guardian Angel* one year after its release:

> The sound of the album is totally different to their recent LPs. Hank's lead guitar work is not always prominent, giving way to a wall of keyboard and synthesiser sound. Brian's drumming at times verges on the monotonous (almost like a disco drum machine!) and the whole album seems to have been recorded in Echo Canyon.

This is somewhat overstated, I think, but it corresponded broadly to the perception of many at the time: in fact, with the dramatic revival of interest in the 1990s once the group was no more, fans were often hunting around not just for the very elusive CD but even for the original LP!

For the group and for Polydor, both of whom were in the business of selling records, the subsequent move to wholly or predominantly chart-based cover Albums was natural and, as events showed, wholly justified. For Shadows fans, whose numbers were already dwindling, it was not good news, not just because The Shadows were not doing what they used to do, but because, not to put too fine a point on it, they were felt to be operating in strictly "alien" territory.

In fact, I am quite sure that there is a sociological aspect to the question. Music for most listeners requires a period of habituation or exposure — we are all familiar with the process of something "growing on" us; we can sometimes be surprised at what we end up liking, or even admiring, after a lukewarm initial impression. At the same time, musical likes and dislikes tend to be developed in the formative years of teens and early 20s. By the 1980s family and other commitments made it quite impracticable for perhaps the majority of the devoted Shadows fans of the 1960s to pay much attention (supposing there was the inclination) to new generation music.

Moving back in conclusion to the question of the chart performance of Shadows' Albums over the years 1980 to 1990, the earlier *Change Of Address, Life In The Jungle* + freebie and *XXV* performed sufficiently well to warrant the assumption that traditional Shadows fans contributed significantly to their commercial success, though a gradual decline in support is perceptible. *Hits Right Up Your Street*, as a "cover" Album first and foremost, bucks the trend, not so much by virtue of its peak position as of its much longer spell as a steady seller (sixteen weeks as opposed to a straight three sixes for the above!). Clearly it was not just or even predominantly hardline Shadows fans operating here.

After *Guardian Angel* we are back with a straight run of essentially cover material (including "self-covers"), carrying on the *Street* tradition; five Albums in the Top Twenty, three of them in particular enjoying long spells in the charts. The highest achiever in terms of peak position was the last, *Reflection*, at Number Five — perhaps pulling in more Shadows fans after the incorporation of half a dozen remakes of 60s/70s material.

Nottingham 1990
Photographs: John Hank Humphrey

INTRODUCTION: III

SHADOWS PERSONNEL

In the 1980s "The Shadows" were strictly speaking a three-man band comprising Hank Marvin, Bruce Welch and Brian Bennett, with others brought in for live appearances and recording as and when, the "others" for the most part being Cliff Hall and Alan Jones.[20] In the latter category, the following divergencies were specified:

1
For the 1980 *Change Of Address* Album and associated Singles (#1–3) add Dave Lawson[21] on synthesisers where apposite (Cliff Hall on piano and Fender Rhodes).
2
The Silver Album (#19): A WHITER SHADE OF PALE has Alan Hawkshaw on keyboards.
3
XXV (#21): THE MODERN WAY Harry Bogdanovs on keyboards; LIVERPOOL DAYS Tony Catchpole on keyboards, with vocal support from Tony Rivers.
4
Guardian Angel (#27): backing vocals from Tony Rivers on GUARDIAN ANGEL, CAN'T PLAY YOUR GAME, ON A NIGHT LIKE THIS.
5
Moonlight Shadows, the twelve fresh tracks (#36): Paul Westwood not Alan Jones on bass guitar.
6
Simply ... Shadows (#44): on THEMES FROM EASTENDERS ..., Mark Griffiths on bass guitar.
7
The Shadows At Their Very Best (#56) and *Reflection* (#59) entire: Mark Griffiths on bass guitar.

---

[20] See Alan Jones in *SCOFA* 35 (1996) 16 for the basic setup.
[21] For an indication of his earlier involvement in recordings see *The Shadows At EMI*, #185 (p. 360), #188 (p.367), #192 (pp. 370–371).

Nottingham 1990
Photograph: John Hank Humphrey

Nottingham 1990
Photograph: John Hank Humphrey

INTRODUCTION: IV

ARRANGEMENT AND PRODUCTION

All primary releases were described as "Arranged and produced by The Shadows", with these exceptions:

• Arranged by The Shadows; produced by Bruce Welch
#18 Single DIAMONDS / ELEVENIS
#19 *The Shadows' Silver Album*, all new tracks (cf. #22 [a-side], #36 [two tracks]) ~ #21 Album *XXV* entire

• Produced by Stuart Coleman
#24 A-Single ON A NIGHT LIKE THIS (also featured on Album #27)

• Remixed by Murray Munro
DANCING IN THE DARK, 7" version (#37 + #91!), 12" version (#38)

Usk 27 September 1990
Photograph: David Hawley

Sheffield 1990
Photograph: John Hank Humphrey

Nottingham 1990
Photograph: John Hank Humphrey

INTRODUCTION: V

UK LABELS AND PICTURE SLEEVES

The following Singles were released with both red and silver labels:

#9 IMAGINE: WOMAN
#12 TREAT ME NICE
#18 DIAMONDS
#22 GOING HOME
#24 ON A NIGHT LIKE THIS

IMAGINE: WOMAN, Silver Label

Picture covers were produced for all but four, which have the standard red/ black / white soft paper covers:

#3 MOZART FORTE
#6 THE THIRD MAN
#7 TELSTAR
#9 IMAGINE: WOMAN

The study of labels, sleeves and so on is a highly specialised one; some work remains to be done, or at least made public. The above represents the barest bones. However, as an example (Les Woosey adds), it is known that many of the picture covers were printed on harder card and/ or soft paper.

Usk 29 September 1990
Photograph: David Hawley

Croydon 18 October 1990
Photograph: David Hawley

ANNUAL SURVEYS, 1980–PRESENT

INGREDIENTS AND LAYOUT

There are entries for vinyl and CD releases as appropriate for the years 1980 through to 2002 (though 1988 and 1995 are both empty years); at the close there is an entry for the solitary DVD released in 2000. No account is taken of bootlegs/ counterfeit recordings.

Each issue is fronted by a **boxed area** specifying month and year of release, main entry reference number (#) in **bold**, format (Single/ LP, CD Single/ CD Album), label + catalogue number, full title(s). All *overseas* releases for a given year are recorded *without* month (these very often could not be ascertained[1], and in most cases probably never will be), and are located together *after* the run of UK releases. Here is an example of the basic scheme:

September 1980 **#3** • Single, Polydor POSP 187 ~ 2059 286[2]: MOZART FORTE / MIDNIGHT CREEPIN'

Under each of the numbered entries, any or all of the following data are provided as appropriate:

• Track-Listing / Composers

Christian names of composers are provided throughout; attribution/ spelling errors in individual releases have been tacitly corrected. The symbol // is used to mark the dividing line between A- and B-sides of LPs.

• Vocal Tracks

An indication of the presence or otherwise on Albums of vocal tracks (rare in the Polydor era).

[1] All the UK months of release bar one are within the discographer's grasp. I have gone to some trouble to provide accurate information (using my own records of CD purchases over the years) among sometimes conflicting data in the main reference works.

[2] This latter is the international number.

• UK Chart Performance
Summary information on date of first chart entry, highest position attained, and number of weeks spent on chart.
• Poll Placings
(a) Top Twenty rankings relating to Polydor material from two polls conducted by *SCOFA* in the years 1985 and 1992.
(b) Top Twenty rankings for two categories in the *Shadsfax* Poll for 2001 (see Preface): "Best Cover" and "Best Instro 1970–1990".
Entries will be found under Albums, not under the Singles sourced from Albums.
• Distribution
The spread of a given release worldwide by country, whether issued in the year of UK release or later.
• Overseas Variations
[Under UK Singles entries]
UK A-/B-sides differently combined, or UK Album tracks used, on overseas Singles.
• Associated Singles
[Under UK Albums entries]
Singles tracks (UK/ overseas) sourced from the UK Albums.
• CD Issues
of the early vinyl-only Albums.
• First Appearance On CD
of all tracks appearing initially on vinyl only.
• Stage Performances
An indication of the relevant numbers performed on stage between the years 1980–1990, based chiefly on the data accumulated by George Geddes in *SCOFA* 24 (1990) 9–12. — Abbreviation used here: George Geddes *On Stage* + page number(s).

There follows extended track analysis and, for Albums, overall assessment; or, for derivative releases, general product descriptions.

Finally, all primary Albums are provided with information on the originals of cover versions: the catalogue number and release date of the relevant Single (nearly always a UK, only rarely a USA Single, or an Album track), and a CD source (chosen on grounds of availability and sound quality wherever practicable).

1980

August 1980

#1

• Single, Polydor POSP 148 ~ 2059 269:

EQUINOXE (PART V) [Edit[3]] / FENDER BENDER

Composers

Side A: Jean-Michel Jarre

Side B: Bruce Welch / Brian Bennett / Hank Marvin

UK Chart Performance

Date of first chart entry: 23 August 1980

Highest position in chart: *50*

Weeks in chart: 3

[3] See *CD Guide* 276.

Distribution

UK, and Australia, France, Germany, Ireland, New Zealand, Scandinavia, Spain

Overseas Variations

#4	INDIGO / FENDER BENDER
#10	EQUINOXE (PART V) [Edit] / ALBATROSS

First Appearance On CD

Side A: *Guardian Angel ... Plus* (UK 1998) 19 (#81)
Side B: *The Shadows Collection* (UK 1989) 11 (#57)

Detail from Back Cover:
uniquely, a date/ venue guide to the Shads tour
(October/ November 1980)

On this, their debut Polydor Single[4], The Shadows carried on with the familiar practice of combining an outside-sourced A-side with a group original on the flipside.[5] For the leading number they turned for inspiration to Jean-Michel Jarre's EQUINOXE (PART V): his suites *Oxygène*[6] and *Equinoxe* had by this time established him as Europe's foremost exponent of electronic

---

[4] On the circumstances surrounding change of label there is a lucid account from Brian Goode in *Shadsfax* 28 [2000] 16.
[5] Viz., an unbroken run of six Singles from August 1978 (LOVE DELUXE / SWEET SATURDAY NIGHT) through to July 1980 (HEART OF GLASS / RETURN TO THE ALAMO, last EMI Single).
[6] OXYGÈNE (PART IV) was to be visited by Hank Marvin on his Album *Heartbeat* (UK No. 17, 1993), see on #2 below.

music. Jarre and Hank Marvin would visit the UK Singles charts together in 1989 when they collaborated on 'London Kid' (Polydor PO 32; peaked at No. 52).[7]

This was an edited version: over 50 seconds shorter than the Album version examined under #2 below (4m 26s[8] from 5m 18s). The chief modification is to be found in the trimming of the most pronounced "electronic" sequence during the second minute[9] — a reduction of close on 50%; also, Bruce Welch's later rhythm guitar break is halved (the reversion to the main theme seems just a bit too abrupt).

The very different FENDER BENDER proved a worthy companion-piece — a mean-sounding boogie enlivened by a slick piano accompaniment and a cleverly structured outro featuring Brian Bennett in APACHE mode set against a sequence of gently strummed chords from Bruce Welch. "Stylistically it was similar to the playing of Jerry Reed. So similar, in fact, that the track was originally going to be called 'Jerry Reed'!" remarks Rob Bradford, sleevenotes to 1998 CD *Shadstrax*.

September 1980

#2

• LP, Polydor Deluxe 2442 179:
Change Of Address

Track Listing / Composers

1 MOZART FORTE
W A Mozart, arr. Bruce Welch / Brian Bennett / Hank Marvin

2 MIDNIGHT CREEPIN'
Bruce Welch / Brian Bennett / Hank Marvin

3 CHANGE OF ADDRESS
Bruce Welch / Brian Bennett / Hank Marvin

4 JUST THE WAY YOU ARE
Billy Joel

[7] Also — and with greater success — on the Album *Revolutions* (UK No. 2, 1988). A further Album, *Jarre Live*, featured Hank on 'London Kid' and 'Rendez-vous IV' (UK No. 16, 1989).
[8] All three CD releases (see Index of Titles) clock in at 4m 19s (shorter fade).
[9] See on #2 below.

5 INDIGO
Dieter Geike / Michael Topolov
6 ARTY'S PARTY
Bruce Welch / Brian Bennett / Hank Marvin //
7 OUTDIGO
Bruce Welch / Brian Bennett / Hank Marvin
8 HELLO MR W.A.M.
W A Mozart, arr. Giorgio Moroder
9 TEMPTATION
Nacio Herb Brown / Arthur Freed
10 ALBATROSS
Peter Green
11 IF YOU LEAVE ME NOW
Peter Cetera
12 EQUINOXE (PART V) [Full Version[10]]
Jean-Michel Jarre

Vocal Tracks
None

UK Chart Performance

Date of first chart entry:	13 September 1980
Highest position in chart:	*17*
Weeks in chart:	6

Top 20 Placing, *SCOFA* Poll (Polydor +) 1985
Top 20 Placing, *SCOFA* Poll (Polydor) 1992
No. 1 EQUINOXE (PART V)

Top 20 Placing, Best Cover, *Shadsfax* Poll (Polydor +) 2001
No. 6 EQUINOXE (PART V)
Top 20 Placing, Best Instro 1970–1990, *Shadsfax* Poll (Polydor +) 2001
No. 2 EQUINOXE (PART V)
No. 13 MOZART FORTE

Distribution
UK (with budget reissue, see #20), and Australia, France, Germany, Greece, Holland (x 2), Italy, Japan, New Zealand, Norway, Spain, Sweden, Yugoslavia

[10] See under #1 above, and also *CD Guide* 276.

Associated Singles

A-side

MOZART FORTE	#3, #5
INDIGO	#4
EQUINOXE (PART V) [but edit, see under #1]	#1, #10

B-side

MIDNIGHT CREEPIN'	#3
CHANGE OF ADDRESS	#43
ARTY'S PARTY	#55
OUTDIGO	#45
TEMPTATION	#5
ALBATROSS	#10

CD Issue

See under #67 below

First Appearance On CD

• *Compact Shadows* (UK 1984, #26)
MOZART FORTE (track 9), HELLO MR W.A.M. (12), IF YOU LEAVE ME NOW (10), EQUINOXE (PART V) (1)

• *Guitars In Love* (Holland 1987, #48)
CHANGE OF ADDRESS (track 13), JUST THE WAY YOU ARE (11), ALBATROSS (4)

• *The Shadows Collection* (UK 1989, #57)
MIDNIGHT CREEPIN' (track 3), TEMPTATION (12)

• CD Single SHADOWMIX (UK 1989, #55)
ARTY'S PARTY (track 2)

• *Dancing In The Dark* (UK 1990/91, #62 + #64)
OUTDIGO (track 11)

• *Change Of Address* (UK 1992, #67)
INDIGO (track 5)

Stage Performances

On the basis of the data assembled by George Geddes, *On Stage* pp. 7–11:

• Their Autumn 1980 UK / European[11] tour took in MOZART FORTE, MIDNIGHT CREEPIN', CHANGE OF ADDRESS, ARTY'S PARTY, TEMPTATION, ALBATROSS, EQUINOXE (PART V).

• Of these the most enduring proved to be the last, regularly performed throughout the decade[12]; also: ARTY'S PARTY recurred in 1982/83/87, TEMPTATION in 1981/82/83/84, ALBATROSS in 1982.

****

At the time that this, the first Polydor LP, hit the shops, the final EMI non-compilation LP, *String Of Hits*, was still a relatively recent memory: though released in August 1979, it actually made No. 1 in March 1980.[13] For *String Of Hits* the three principal members of the group composed only SONG FOR DUKE, a piece which reportedly started life with the working title of THE NORWEGIANS[14], but was renamed to replace a further derivative number, BLACK IS BLACK, at the last moment, as a tribute to the recently deceased John Wayne[15]. To all intents and purposes however, the Album was true to its name, offering "cover" material with a broad appeal.

The emphasis on *Change Of Address* was different. On offer this time were four brand-new, original and varied compositions, all from the trio Marvin Welch & Bennett:

• **MIDNIGHT CREEPIN'**, "a slinky stalker of a number" in Rob Bradford's words[16], with Hank's fluent lead set off by a distinctive bassline from Alan Jones.

• The elegant **CHANGE OF ADDRESS**, its general ambience reminiscent of ALBATROSS (below), perhaps evoking an image of a tranquil, untroubled transition to pastures new?

• **ARTY'S PARTY**, one of those infectious toe-tappers at which The Shadows excelled, and funky with it!

---

11 Cf. Tony Hoffman in *Shadsfax* 3 (1996) 22, on the set put on by The Shadows at The Mogador, Paris.

12 Also in 1990: see the reports in *SCOFA* 25 (1990) 4 and 26 (1991) 14–15.

13 See *The Shadows At EMI* 361 for a sketch of its progress.

14 *Shadsfax* 31 [2001] 8–9.

15 *The Shadows At EMI* 370, note 1.

16 Sleeve notes to 1998 CD *Shadstrax*.

• **OUTDIGO**, an up-tempo, and loose, variation on the German-sourced INDIGO (below), conjuring up an entirely different mood, quite at variance with its introspective prototype. The musical content is definitely superior to the word-play! Hanks's flowing lead is effectively complemented by a lively rockabilly piano accompaniment from Cliff Hall.

To turn to **INDIGO** next: this instrumental was recorded by the German group Blonker in 1977, when it attracted a lot of air-play. As its title suggests, it is a moody piece, performed with a full, resonant soundstage. The Shadows' version is rather less emotionally charged — drier in texture with a less full-bodied sound overall.

Many instrumental groups in the 1960s seized upon familiar classical compositions, as often as not vulgarising them by giving them a raucous edge. Not so The Shadows, who had seldom dipped into this bottomless pool. Under Norrie Paramor's watchful gaze they issued a supremely controlled and tuneful version of Franz Liszt's A SIGH[17] on the 1966 Album *Shadow Music*. On the 1979 *String Of Hits* they included an elegant rendition of a more recent "classic", a movement from Rodrigo's famous 'Concerto de Aranjuez'. Virtuoso classical guitarist John Williams had had an Album in the Top Twenty with this Concerto in 1976, and was enjoying success (in addition to his 'Cavatina' Single in 1979 alongside The Shadows' THEME FROM THE DEER HUNTER) as a member of the classical/jazz/rock fusion group Sky, with a hit Single (derived from Bach) and a hit Album (their second) earlier in 1980. The Shadows for their part turned their attention to the sublime compositions of Wolfgang Amadeus Mozart (one of them to serve as an A-Single, see #3), though in both cases there were notable forerunners, one recent, one not so recent:

HELLO MR W.A.M. was a reworking by synthesiser exponent (and composer) Giorgio Moroder, for the soundtrack (end-titles) of the 1980 movie 'American Gigolo'[18], of Clarinet Concerto in A Major K. 622, 2nd Movement (Adagio). The Shadows' version is brilliantly executed: a beautiful, soothing melody, interrupted in mid-course by a dazzling up-tempo tour de force (this a Moroder importation!) — Mozart and beat-group perfectly united.

---

[17] 'Un sospero', from his 1848 *Concert Studies*.

[18] The soundtrack Album had made the American Top Ten earlier in 1980, while Blondie's song from the film, 'Call Me', had been a chart-topper either side of the Atlantic.

The other adaptation, **MOZART FORTE**, is a variation on MOZART FORTY, viz. the 1st Movement of Symphony No. 40 in G Minor, K. 550 (Allegro Molto). The Argentine bandleader Waldo de los Rios specialised in pepping up the classics[19], working his way from the 1950s to the 1980s through Bach, Beethoven, Chopin and others; he had invested this stupendous creation with a guitar accompaniment and a lively rhythm section on his hit Single of 1971 (it reached No. 5).[20] The Shadows storm their way through this piece and make it their own.

A further instrumental success, and a bigger hit in the field of popular music, was Fleetwood Mac's first million-seller, **ALBATROSS**, a haunting and evocative guitar opus which derived much of its effect from a distant slide guitar and resounding cymbals. ALBATROSS enjoyed the distinction of soaring to Number One in January 1969 *and* to Number Two in June 1973. Comparisons are interesting. Although the basic arrangements are very similar, the lead guitar on The Shadows' version has a clinical sound, lacking the distinct "bloom" of the Peter Green original, while the accompaniment has a markedly "processed" character — a true product of the 1980s in fact. As an example of a Shadows' "soundscape" it is comprehensively outclassed by BERMUDA TRIANGLE (on the 1977 LP *Tasty*).

An instrumental of a far different kind provided *Change Of Address* with a rousing finale. Jean-Michel Jarre's *Equinoxe* Album hit No. 11 in the UK charts of 1979, going on to sell several million copies worldwide. (The sourced Single, **EQUINOXE (PART V)**, made less of an impact, peaking at No. 45). Nothing like the bewilderingly rich electronic tapestry of Jarre's original is reproduced by The Shadows.[21] It is transformed by them into a straightforward though blistering guitar instro with a rippling if relatively restrained keyboard accompaniment.[22] In fact, "EQUINOXE (PART V)" is something of a misnomer. Over the 5m 18s taken up by this track, themes from Parts VI and VII of this opus are also worked in, to fine effect.

The remaining three tunes on *Change Of Address* are more familiar as vocals. All were outstanding commercial successes. I recall a well-informed record

---

19 Arrangement credited to Ellis Rich and Ben Kelsey.

20 A 'Mozart Forty' was also offered by The Ventures on their 1972 LP *Joy (The Ventures Play The Classics)*.

21 The closest approximation is to be found in the sequence from 2m 01s to 2m 53s: but this is pretty tame stuff by Jarre's standards.

22 Much more adventurous, over a decade further on, is the approach on Hank Marvin's OXYGÈNE (PART IV) (see on #1 above), both in the lead guitar part and in the accompaniment.

retailer in Edinburgh emphasising to me, when discussing this latest Shadows' Album, that for the casual buyer of instrumental LPs (of which he encountered a fair number), the presence of even two or three "well known hits" made all the difference — a point that Polydor was to take to its logical conclusion for much of The Shadows' association with the label.

The earliest of the three is **TEMPTATION**. The closest vocal counterpart to The Shadows' rendition (Bing Crosby's belongs to a different world[23]) was of course The Everly Brothers' no-holds-barred Number One Single of 1961. TEMPTATION provides a rare example of a studio remake by the group of a non-Single track. A stunning version had appeared on the 1964 LP *Dance With The Shadows*. The new take furnishes as good a contrast as any between the "old" and the "new", 1980s, Shadows' sound. A prominent feature of the 1960's cut was Bruce Welch's driving acoustic rhythm accompaniment, so skilfully executed that the music seemed to take on a momentum of its own. Energetic as the fresh version is, it possesses a more rigid and formalised structure, and is most certainly a product of the "synthetic" approach to music-making.

A second chart-topping vocal Single (this time on the other side of the Atlantic too) represented here in instrumental dress was Chicago's tuneful ballad **IF YOU LEAVE ME NOW** from 1976. The sound is warm and mellow, uninfluenced by the shrill, forced vocal delivery of the original.

Finally, a technically flawless but rather languid rendition of Billy Joel's romantic ballad (his first UK hit, in 1978), **JUST THE WAY YOU ARE** — the most familiar piece on his hugely popular Album (No. 2 in the USA) *The Stranger*. Here was a song destined to attract a host of cover versions — to become an MOR "standard" in fact. Joel stalled at No. 19 in the UK charts (he hit No. 3 in his native country); he was outdone here by Barry White (whose version peaked at No. 12) in the course of his run of fourteen hit Singles during the 1970s.

The Shadows, armed with a new recording contract, made no attempt to flood this sequel to the hugely successful *String Of Hits* with relatively recent material to which the record-buying public, whose chief interest was in vocals, could immediately relate — the Billy Joel and Chicago pieces alone

---

[23] A serene piece as conceived by Freed and Brown ("noted Hollywood contract-composers" in Jim Nugent's words), creators of the likes of 'All I Do Is Dream Of You', 'Singin' In The Rain' and 'You Were Meant For Me'.

come into that category. In fact, the best tracks are the reworkings of the instrumentals MOZART FORTE, INDIGO, HELLO MR W.A.M., EQUINOXE (PART V); together with the group originals, particularly MIDNIGHT CREEPIN' and OUTDIGO.

Although *Change Of Address* was reissued as a budget LP in 1983 (#20), Polydor did not put the Album out on CD until 1992 (#67), and then with the bare minimum of effort expended on documentation and even on artwork; their *Compact Shadows* of 1984 (#26) netted only four of the tracks, but Pickwick in three discs sold as a set in 1990 (see #62) scooped up as many as ten. Long since deleted, another, more considered, release of this fine Album would be most welcome to Shadows' fans.

Originals Of Cover Versions

• MOZART FORTE
UK Single:
Waldo de los Rios,
'Mozart Symphony No. 40
in G Minor, First Movement',
A & M AMS 836 (1971)
CD:
Music And Romance,
Disky INS 857092,
track 3 (1999)

• JUST THE WAY YOU ARE
UK Single:
Billy Joel, CBS 5872 (1978)
CD:
The Ultimate Collection, Columbia Sony TV98CD, Disc 1/1 (2000)
UK Single:
Barry White, 20th Century BTC 2380 (1978)
CD:
The Collection, Universal Music TV 834 790–2, track 5 (2000)

• INDIGO
CD:
Blonker,
Die Zeit der Träume,
Mercury 826 932–2 Q,
track 9 (n.d.)

• HELLO MR W.A.M.
CD:
Soundtrack *American Gigolo*,
Spectrum 551 103–2,
track 4 (1999)

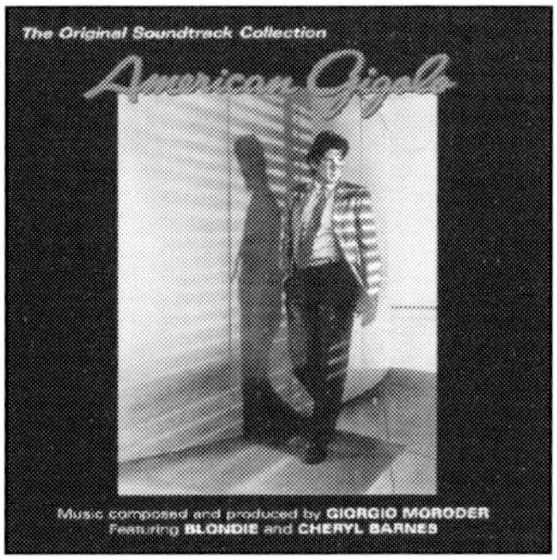

• TEMPTATION
UK Single:
The Everly Brothers, Warner Bros WB 42 (1961)
CD:
The Definitive Everly Brothers, WSM 0927 47304–2, Disc 1/24 (2002)

• ALBATROSS
UK Single:
Fleetwood Mac, Blue Horizon 57 3145 (1968); reissue CBS 8306 (1973)
CD:
The Very Best Of Fleetwood Mac, Warner Brothers 8122 73635 2, track 6 (2002)

• IF YOU LEAVE ME NOW
UK Single:
Chicago, CBS 4603 (1976)
CD:
The Chicago Story — The Complete Greatest Hits,
Rhino/WSM 8122 73630 2, track 1 (2002)

• EQUINOXE (PART V)
UK Single:
Jean-Michel Jarre,
Polydor POSP 20 (1979)
CD:
Equinoxe,
Dreyfus 487376 2,
track 5
(and tracks 6/7, see analysis above)
(1997)

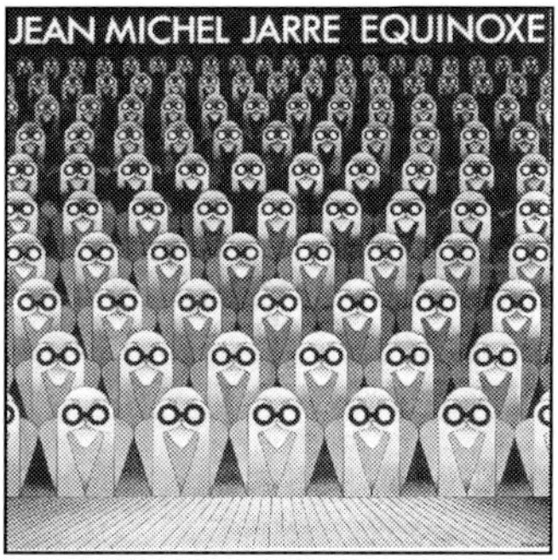

September 1980

#3

• Single, Polydor POSP 187 ~ 2059 286:
MOZART FORTE / MIDNIGHT CREEPIN'

Composers
Side A: W A Mozart, arr. Bruce Welch / Brian Bennett / Hank Marvin
Side B: Bruce Welch / Brian Bennett / Hank Marvin

Distribution
UK, and Holland, Spain

Overseas Variation
#5 MOZART FORTE / TEMPTATION

First Appearance On CD
Side A: *Compact Shadows* (UK 1984) 9 (#26)
Side B: *The Shadows Collection* (UK 1989) 3 (#57)

The first two tracks of the newly released LP *Change Of Address*, "issued to tie in with the group's autumn tour" (Rob Bradford, *Record Collector* 124 (December 1989): *Singles 1973–89*, 78); both numbers were performed on stage, see on #2 above. MOZART FORTE was taken on board by Bruce Welch's Shadows at Shadowmania 2001, see the report in *Shadsfax* 33 [2001] 13; it looks set to become a "regular": id. 35 [2002] 18.

1980

#4

• Overseas Single, Polydor 2059 289:
INDIGO / FENDER BENDER

Issued in Belgium and Holland. A variation on the EQUINOXE (PART V) / FENDER BENDER pairing from August 1980 (#1), this A-side highlighting the contribution of the German group Blonker (see under #2).

1980

#5

• Overseas Single, Polydor POL 22036 (33 rpm):
MOZART FORTE / TEMPTATION

Issued in Bolivia. A variation on MOZART FORTE / MIDNIGHT CREEPIN' (#3), the original composition of the B-side being dropped in favour of a thoroughly familiar number (similarly with the overseas Singles under #10 and #46 below).

****

**The group toured extensively in the 80s.
This is an exterior shot of
The Hammersmith Odeon in 1989.
Photograph: John Hank Humphrey.**

1981

April 1981

#6

• Single, Polydor POSP 255:
THE THIRD MAN / THE FOURTH MAN

Composers
Side A: Anton Karas
Side B: Hank Marvin / Bruce Welch / Brian Bennett

UK Chart Performance
Date of first chart entry: 2 May 1981
Highest position in chart: *44*
Weeks in chart: 4
• The Shadows' last charting Single

Distribution
UK, and Belgium, France, Holland, Ireland, New Zealand, Portugal, Scandinavia, South Africa, Spain

First Appearance On CD
Side A: *Compact Shadows* (UK 1984) 2 (#26)
Side B: *The Shadows Collection* (UK 1989) 13 (#57)

****

For the A-side see on #8. The original flipside is one of those easy-going jazz-tinged instrumentals at which the group excelled — the working title in fact was 'The Jazzy One' (Rob Bradford, sleeve notes to 1998 CD *Shadstrax*).

August 1981
#7
• Single, Polydor POSP 316:
TELSTAR / SUMMER LOVE '59

Composers
Side A: Joe Meek
Side B: Hank Marvin / Bruce Welch / Brian Bennett

Distribution
UK, and France

Overseas Variation
#11 CHI MAI / SUMMER LOVE '59

First Appearance On CD
Side A: *Hits Right Up Your Street* (UK 1987) 1 (#42)
Side B: *Compact Shadows* (UK 1984) 11 (#26)

****

Both numbers were to put in an appearance shortly on the LP *Hits Right Up Your Street* (see #8). THE THIRD MAN had charted in May (with no promotion from the group), so another instrumental of good pedigree must have seemed worth trying: but The Shadows' days in the Singles charts, as already noted, were now over.

September 1981
#8
• LP, Polydor POLD 5046 ~ 2442 194:
Hits Right Up Your Street

Track-Listing / Composers
1 TELSTAR
Joe Meek
2 CHI MAI
Ennio Morricone

3 WE DON'T TALK ANYMORE
Alan Tarney
4 IMAGINE : WOMAN
John Lennon
5 HATS OFF TO WALLY
Hank Marvin / Bruce Welch / Brian Bennett
6 ONE DAY I'LL FLY AWAY
Will Jennings / Joe Sample
7 SUMMER LOVE '59
Hank Marvin / Bruce Welch / Brian Bennett
8 MISTY
Erroll Garner //
9 THIS OLE HOUSE
Stuart Hamblen
10 THE WINNER TAKES IT ALL
Benny Andersson / Björn Ulvaeus
11 SAILING
Gavin Sutherland
12 THING-ME-JIG
Hank Marvin / Bruce Welch / Brian Bennett
13 MORE THAN I CAN SAY
Sonny Curtis / Jerry Allison
14 COWBOY CAFE
Hank Marvin / Bruce Welch / Brian Bennett
15 THE THIRD MAN
Anton Karas
16 NUT ROCKER
Kim Fowley (with some [uncredited] input from Tchaikovsky)

Vocal Tracks
None

UK Chart Performance

Date of first chart entry:	19 September 1981
Highest position in chart:	*15*
Weeks in chart:	16

Top 20 Placing, *SCOFA* Poll (Polydor +) 1985

No. 14 THE THIRD MAN
No. 15 CHI MAI

Top 20 Placing, *SCOFA* Poll (Polydor) 1992

No. 10 SUMMER LOVE '59

No. 16 THING-ME-JIG

Distribution

UK (with budget reissue August 1984, see #25), and Australia, France, Germany, Holland, Israel, Italy, Japan, New Zealand (x 2), Norway, South Africa, Spain, Yugoslavia

Associated Singles

A-side	
TELSTAR	#7
CHI MAI	#11
IMAGINE: WOMAN	#9
THE THIRD MAN	#6
B-side	
HATS OFF TO WALLY	#9
SUMMER LOVE '59	#7, #11
THING-ME-JIG	#24

CD Issues

See below, #42 and #68

First Appearance On CD

• *Hits Right Up Your Street* (UK 1987, #42), except:-

• *Compact Shadows* (UK 1984, #26)

CHI MAI (track 5), SUMMER LOVE '59 (11), SAILING (17), THING-ME-JIG (7), MORE THAN I CAN SAY (14), THE THIRD MAN (2)

• *Moonlight Shadows* (UK 1986, #36)

IMAGINE: WOMAN (track 15)

Stage Performances

On the basis of the data assembled by George Geddes, *On Stage* pp. 7–11:

• NUT ROCKER was commonly featured, initially at least, 1980/81/82/83/87, as also THE THIRD MAN 1981/82/83, and CHI MAI 1981/83/84.

• TELSTAR and IMAGINE: WOMAN were performed in 1981; and (but as a *vocal*) MORE THAN I CAN SAY in 1980 (sic).

On this Album, as on *Change Of Address*, four original compositions were interspersed with derivative material:

• HATS OFF TO WALLY
"Wally" not "Larry" as per Del Shannon; an exuberant toe-tapper which bounces along much in the manner of COTTON PICKIN' on the 1965 LP *The Sound Of The Shadows*, this with a lively rockabilly piano accompaniment from Cliff Hall.

• SUMMER LOVE '59
A genial and melodious throwback to the "time to dim the lights" of youth-clubs in the late 50s / early 60s. Bruce Welch's rhythm guitar provides an effective backdrop.

• THING-ME-JIG
Resonant keyboards and guitars combine to produce a spirited slant on a genre seldom exploited by the smaller-scale instro bands. Entertaining.

• COWBOY CAFE
Like every society, the Wild West had its serene and even genteel side, reflected it would seem in this tuneful piece — far removed from the boisterous atmosphere of the saloon bar!

Definitely out on its own in this set is **THE THIRD MAN**, a Fender-led (and reggae-orientated) account of the haunting 'The Third Man Theme' from the classic 1949 movie, brilliantly performed by zither maestro Anton Karas. Atmosphere there is none, but the ever resourceful Alan Jones breathes new life into the original's rather deliberate bassline.

The remaining eleven tracks certainly live up to the Album's title in that, in UK chart terms, seven Number Ones and four Number Twos are called up, spanning three decades.

Representatives from the 1960s, aptly enough, are two chart-topping instrumentals. The more illustrious of the two, The Tornados' **TELSTAR**, hit Number One on 4 October 1962 (and later in the year Stateside as well), dominating the instrumental field between GUITAR TANGO and DANCE ON! The Shadows offer a driving, uplifting guitar-led version, divested of the various extraneous sound-effects of the original — and with a decent dynamic range into the bargain! A closing reference to "Also Sprach Zarathustra", with its "extra-terrestrial" associations, lends a novel touch.

In contrast, the new version of B Bumble and The Stingers' **NUT ROCKER**, another Number One from 1962 (it took over from WONDERFUL LAND on 17 May), is handled too deliberately, lacking as it does the raw edge and sheer ebullience which render the original — an outrageous all-out assault on Tchaikovsky's 'Nutcracker Suite' — so irresistible.[24]

Moving on to material inspired by hits of the 1970s:-

The standard **MISTY** had been performed by a number of artists in a variety of styles, but behind The Shadows' superbly swinging version lies Ray Stevens' bluegrass-tinged Number Two Single from 1975 — and hugely enjoyable it is too. One of the best tracks on the Album.

A chart-topper that same year was Rod Stewart's anthemic **SAILING**. A cynic might wonder however how the man behind 'Maggie May' and 'You Wear It Well' came to record such a desperately laboured song. It fares no better as an instrumental, and certainly outstays its welcome at close on 5m.

The third and last hit covered from this decade is Cliff Richard's 1979 **WE DON'T TALK ANYMORE**, his first Number One since 'Congratulations' in 1968 — a superlative song with passionately delivered lyrics and sparkling accompaniment. The Shadows' version is smooth-flowing[25] rather than expressive, though it comes to life towards the close (3m 15s on) with the injection of some slick variations from Hank on the basic melody.

The remaining six tracks consist of cover versions of chart material from 1980–1981.

IMAGINE was not new to the UK charts: it climbed to No. 6 in 1975; but it provided John Lennon, in the wake of his brutal murder in December 1980, with a second posthumous Number One, early in 1981; **WOMAN** followed shortly after to complete a hat-trick. Although IMAGINE with its idealistic lyrics has received more plaudits, WOMAN too proved that Lennon's awesome melodic inventiveness had by no means deserted him in the post-Beatles' years. The Shadows' sensitively performed medley turned out to be

---

[24] On B Bumble's creations: Dave Burke, *Pipeline* 28 (1995) 41: "brash, almost [?] vulgar piano-led adaptations of well known classical themes ..." (my brackets).

[25] Alan Taylor's description "plodding" maybe goes a bit too far (*Pipeline* 8 [1991] 16).

a fine tribute to a member of a group that used to include APACHE in their repertoire in the course of 1960.[26]

With their eighth chart-topper (in 1980), a younger supergroup, Abba, provided one of the high spots on *Hits Right Up Your Street*. **THE WINNER TAKES IT ALL**, one of Agnetha Fältskog's finest vocal performances, is turned into an instrumental of the highest quality, the changes of tempo managed to perfection — and what a bassline! What a pity The Shadows did not call upon Abba's rich catalogue more often in the 80s.

Our final Number One of the survey, from 1981, was a revival of a song of the 1940s. The bouncy **THIS OLE HOUSE**, taken into the higher reaches of our charts by both Rosemary Clooney and Billie Anthony in 1954, was given a specifically rock/ rockabilly treatment by producer Stuart Coleman for Shakin' Stevens — a treatment mirrored in the animated version on this Album.

A trio of Number Twos from 1980/81 remain to be considered. By far the most impressive is the riveting version of Ennio Morricone's **CHI MAI** from the BBC TV series 'The Life And Times Of David Lloyd George'.[27] Morricone's arrangement is followed closely, but Hank softens the shrill string-tone of the original (see further on #11 below).

In the wake of her dazzling contribution to The Crusaders' epic 'Street Life' of 1979, Randy Crawford made the big time here in her own right in 1980 with the Sample-Jennings ballad **ONE DAY I'LL FLY AWAY**. The Shadows' version, though impeccably arranged, is arguably just too laid-back given the intensity of Crawford's vocal delivery and its incisive accompaniment. On the other hand, one critic commended this as "a beautiful 'modern jazz' interpretation": an illustration of how perceptions of music can vary.

---

[26] A further Lennon release, JEALOUS GUY, was adopted on the 1987 LP/CD *Simply Shadows* (#44). Surprisingly few of the 180–odd Beatles' recordings were taken up by The Shadows: PAPERBACK WRITER, GET BACK and George Harrison's SOMETHING on the 1970 LP *Shades Of Rock*; HEY JUDE on *Moonlight Shadows* (#36); STRAWBERRY FIELDS FOREVER on *Reflection* (#59). Hank Marvin would add ELEANOR RIGBY (1997 CD *Hank Plays Live*, 2002 CD *Guitar Player*), A HARD DAY'S NIGHT (2000 CD *Marvin At The Movies*) and TICKET TO RIDE (2002 CD *Guitar Player*); and also Paul McCartney's post-Beatles LIVE AND LET DIE (1993 CD *Heartbeat*).

[27] In fact, the tune was composed originally for an Italian movie, 'Maddalena': see *Record Collector* No. 270 (February 2002) 109.

The final number in this review could hardly fail to appeal to devotees of the Fender guitar and one of its most distinguished exponents — an effortlessly flowing rendition of the Bobby Vee hit **MORE THAN I CAN SAY**, which Leo Sayer, supported by Alan Tarney and Trevor Spencer, had taken to Number Two (both here and in the USA) in 1980.[28]

Taken overall, *Hits Right Up Your Street* is a fine Album, highlighting the group's versatility. The four "originals", accomplished as they are, do not by any means tower above the rest of the set: a number of the derivative pieces — notably MISTY, THE WINNER TAKES IT ALL, CHI MAI and MORE THAN I CAN SAY — demonstrated that the sophisticated guitar-led instro was still alive and well in the early 1980s.

In terms of chart position, *Hits Right Up Your Street* did slightly better than *Change Of Address*; in terms of number of weeks in the charts, it did significantly better: the next Album to match it in this respect would be one with no "originals" at all — *Moonlight Shadows* in 1986. And so, when it came to Polydor putting out back catalogue in CD format, *Change* ... lagged behind *Hits* ... by a clear five years (cf. on #2).

Originals Of Cover Versions

• **TELSTAR**
UK Single:
The Tornados, Decca F 11494 (1962)
CD:
Ridin' The Wind, Castle CMDDD 428, Disc 1/3 (2002)

• **CHI MAI**
UK Single:
Ennio Morricone, BBC RESL 92 (1981)
CD:
The Very Best Of Ennio Morricone, Virgin CDV 2929 (7243 8 50242 2 1), track 4 (2000)

---

[28] Hank Marvin would play on the Sayer-Tarney composition 'Don't Wait Until Tomorrow', one of the tracks on the former's 1983 Album (which peaked at No. 15) *Have You Ever Been In Love*; a year later he would guest on Shakin' Stevens' [see above] Single 'Teardrops' (which climbed to No. 5).

• WE DON'T TALK ANYMORE
UK Single:
Cliff Richard, EMI 2975 (1979)
CD:
The Whole Story — His Greatest Hits, EMI 7243 5 29322 2 1, Disc 1/25 (2000)

• IMAGINE: WOMAN
UK Singles:
(IMAGINE) John Lennon,
Apple R 6009 (re-release 1980);
(WOMAN) Geffen K 79195 (1981)
CD:
Lennon Legend:
The Very Best Of John Lennon,
EMI 7243 8 21954 2 9,
tracks 1 & 13 (1997)

• ONE DAY I'LL FLY AWAY
UK Single:
Randy Crawford, Warner Bros K 17680 (1980)
CD:
The Very Best Of Randy Crawford, Warner.esp. WMM CD 002, track 1 (2000)

• MISTY
UK Single:
Ray Stevens, Janus 6146 204 (1975)
CD:
The Very Best Of Ray Stevens: Misty, Music Club MCCD 401, track 22 (1999)

• THIS OLE HOUSE
UK Single:
Shakin' Stevens,
Epic EPC 9555 (1981)
CD:
The Hits Of Shakin' Stevens,
Epic 466265–2,
track 1 (1996)

• THE WINNER TAKES IT ALL
UK Single:
Abba,
Epic EPC 8835 (1980)
CD:
The Definitive Collection,
Polar 549 974–2,
Disc 2/5 (2001)

• SAILING
UK Single:
Rod Stewart, Warner Bros K 16600 (1975)
CD:
The Story So Far: The Very Best Of Rod Stewart, Warner Bros 8122–73581–2, Disc 2/1 (2001)

• MORE THAN I CAN SAY
UK Single:
Leo Sayer, Chrysalis CHS 2442 (1980)
CD:
The Definitive Hits Collection, Polygram TV 547 115–2, track 14 (1999)

• THE THIRD MAN ('The Harry Lime Theme')
CD:
Soundtrack 'The Third Man', Disconforme SFCD 33538, track 2 (1999)

• NUT ROCKER
UK Single:
B Bumble and The Stingers, Top Rank JAR 611 (1962; 1972: Stateside SS 2203)
CD:
Nut Rocker, Ace CDCHD 577, track 1 (1995)

November 1981

#9

• Single, Polydor POSP 376:
IMAGINE : WOMAN / HATS OFF TO WALLY

Composers
Side A: John Lennon
Side B: Hank Marvin / Bruce Welch / Brian Bennett

Distribution
UK only [2 diff. labels]

First Appearance On CD
Side A: *Moonlight Shadows* (UK 1986), 15 (#36)
Side B: *Hits Right Up Your Street* (UK 1987), 5 (#42)

****

Another couple taken from *Hits Right Up Your Street*, see on #8. A number of John Lennon tributes would make the charts (most notably Roxy Music's 'Jealous Guy', in March), but this was one of the exceptions.

1981

#10

• Overseas Single, Polydor 2059 309:
EQUINOXE (PART V) [Edit] / ALBATROSS

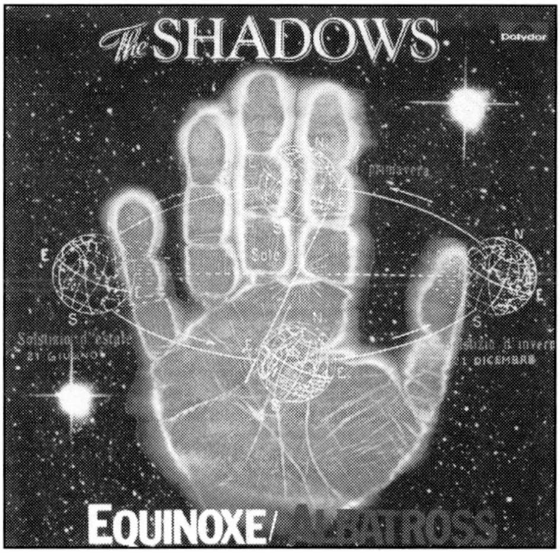

Issued in Italy. A variation, late in the day, on #1 above; on the B-side see #2.

1981

#11

• Overseas Single, Polydor 2059 435:
CHI MAI / SUMMER LOVE '59

Issued in Holland (contrast UK/ France at #7, TELSTAR as A-side). The Shadows' version of CHI MAI compared very favourably with that of Ennio Morricone (see on #8), who had made second place in the charts earlier in the year; a UK release from the group might just have paid off.

1982

May 1982

#12

• Single, Polydor POSP 439 ~ 2059 497:
TREAT ME NICE / SPOT THE BALL

Composers

Side A: Jerry Leiber / Mike Stoller
Side B: Bruce Welch / Brian Bennett / Hank Marvin

Distribution

UK [2 different labels], and Scandinavia

First Appearance On CD

Side A: *Life In The Jungle* (UK 1989) 4 (#52)
Side B: *Dancing In The Dark* (UK 1990/91) 12 (#62/ #64)

On TREAT ME NICE, the group's first vocal A-side since LOVE DELUXE in August 1978, see #14. The excellent SPOT THE BALL, as its title suggests, is a thrusting number in "Match Of The Day" vein; it was submitted as a contender for the World Cup theme according to Brian Bennett (sleevenotes to 1998 CD *Shadstrax*).

July 1982

#13

• Single, Polydor POSP 485:
THEME FROM MISSING / THE SHADY LADY

Note
A 12" Single (Polydor 2812 125), France 1982, but not for sale, is noted in Bernard Broche's Discography (though, apparently, nowhere else).

Composers

Side A: Vangelis
Side B: Hank Marvin / Bruce Welch / Brian Bennett

Top 20 Placing, *SCOFA* Poll (Polydor) 1992

No. 20 THE SHADY LADY

Distribution
UK, and Australia, France, Germany, Holland, Italy, Japan, New Zealand, Portugal, Scandinavia, Spain

First Appearance On CD
Side A: *Compact Shadows* (UK 1984) 8 (#26)
Side B: *The Shadows Collection* (UK 1989) 4 (#57)

****

On the A-side see #14. There never was a Vangelis Single of THEME FROM MISSING (in fact no release of any kind until 1989), so here was a gap to be filled; The Shadows' version however failed to penetrate the Top 75.

THE SHADY LADY may have been inspired by "a boat that someone owned" (Brian Bennett in sleevenotes to 1998 CD *Shadstrax*). If so, a serene cruise is suggested, punctuated by brisker progress at 1m 12s and 2m 08s.

September 1982

#14

• LP, Polydor SHADS 1 ~ 2478 163:
Life In The Jungle

Track Listing / Composers

1 LIFE IN THE JUNGLE
Bruce Welch / Hank Marvin / Brian Bennett
2 HIGH NOON
Dimitri Tiomkin / Ned Washington
3 THEME FROM MISSING
Vangelis
4 TREAT ME NICE
Jerry Leiber / Mike Stoller
5 CAT 'N' MOUSE
Bruce Welch / Hank Marvin / Brian Bennett
6 CHARIOTS OF FIRE
Vangelis //
7 NO DANCING!
Bruce Welch / Hank Marvin / Brian Bennett

8 RIDERS OF THE RANGE
Martin Jenner
9 THE OLD ROMANTICS
Bruce Welch / Hank Marvin / Brian Bennett
10 YOU RESCUE ME
Bruce Welch / Hank Marvin / Brian Bennett / Warren Bennett
11 LILI MARLENE
Norbert Schultze / Hans Leip
12 RAUNCHY
Sidney Manker / Bill Justis

Vocal Tracks
4, 10

UK Chart Performance

Date of first chart entry:	25 September 1982
Highest position in chart:	*24*
Weeks in chart:	6

Top 20 Placing, *SCOFA* Poll (Polydor +) 1985

No. 7	CHARIOTS OF FIRE
No. 12	RIDERS OF THE RANGE
No. 20	LIFE IN THE JUNGLE

Distribution
UK [with reissue 1983 and (see #30) budget reissue 1985], and: Australia, France, Germany, Holland, Japan, New Zealand, Norway, South Africa, Spain

Associated Singles
A-side

THEME FROM MISSING	#13
TREAT ME NICE	#12
CHARIOTS OF FIRE	#16

B-side

LIFE IN THE JUNGLE	#16
CAT 'N' MOUSE	#22
NO DANCING!	#39

CD Issues
See #52 and #69

First Appearance On CD
• *Life In The Jungle* (UK 1989, #52), except:
• *Compact Shadows* (UK 1984, #26)
LIFE IN THE JUNGLE (track 15), THEME FROM MISSING (8), CHARIOTS OF FIRE (16), NO DANCING! (3)

Stage Performances
On the basis of the data assembled by George Geddes, *On Stage* pp. 7–11:
• CHARIOTS OF FIRE proved the most popular (1981/82/83/84/85/87).[29]
• Others hit the stage in 1982/83 (THEME FROM MISSING, TREAT ME NICE, NO DANCING!, RIDERS OF THE RANGE), or in 1982 (LIFE IN THE JUNGLE).

****

Hank Marvin had charted earlier in the year with his solo LP *Words & Music* and the Single 'Don't Talk', peaking at No. 66 and No. 49 respectively. *Life In The Jungle* fared appreciably better. It contained five new group compositions, together with a first-rate contribution from guitarist Martin Jenner, who worked with Cliff Richard in the 1980s[30]: his **RIDERS OF THE RANGE**, harking back to the 1950's radio series of that name[31], is a highly polished equivalent of the sort of "western" themes the group exploited so successfully on their best-selling EP *The Shadows* (1961). Jenner would go on to compose with Hank Marvin some excellent instros for the latter's Albums *Into The Light* (1992) and *Heartbeat* (1993).

The enigmatically titled **LIFE IN THE JUNGLE** and the convoluted **CAT 'N' MOUSE** are not the most incisive of the group's compositions. They are overshadowed by **THE OLD ROMANTICS** (a mellifluous ballad in the best Shadows' tradition, harbouring a self-mocking reference to the *New* Romantics of the 1980s) and by the funky **NO DANCING!** (a tongue-in-cheek title, given that the track is a fair reflection of early 80's dance music[32], or at least certain strands of it). **YOU RESCUE ME** in contrast is a lively vocal that

29 Also in 1990: see the report in *SCOFA* 26 (1991) 14–15.
30 More on him from your roving Fascinating and Frivolous Facts Man (aka George Geddes) in *SCOFA* 5 (1983) 13.
31 To be more precise, it ran from 1949 to 1953, each episode ending memorably with the bark of Rustler the dog!
32 See Brian Bennett quoted in Rob Bradford's sleevenotes to 1998 CD *Shadstrax*.

owes more than a little (whether consciously or not) to the Tarney-Spencer band — a hard act to follow, but this is a pretty creditable effort. Sadly, Shadows' vocals were in short supply in this last phase of their recording career.

The residual six tracks are an interesting mix (not a single UK Number One in sight this time). **LILI MARLENE** is certainly the most surprising inclusion: whether the 1980 film 'Lili Marleen', which recounts how a third-class cabaret singer's recording[33] becomes a hit in Nazi Germany, had any bearing on its choice, I do not know. No matter: this is a track to savour with its stunningly vibrant lead guitar advancing with intricate steps to a steady marching rhythm.[34] A track with real character.

Moving on to a more enlightened decade, **HIGH NOON**, the title song of the 1952 movie, was performed by Tex Ritter, though it was Frankie Laine[35] who took it to No. 7 in our charts. The Shadows transform it into a cracking instrumental, with Hank going into free flight from 2m 07s on. Fans stuck in a 1960's "beat group" groove should have nothing to complain of here!

A second retrospective from the 1950s is Elvis' **TREAT ME NICE**, the A-side of which, 'Jailhouse Rock', hit Number One in 1958; the rousing lead vocal and splendid guitar solo from Hank, the Jordanaires-styled backing vocals, and the 80's ambience make a winning combination.

Finally from the 50s, an ultra-refined version of the Bill Justis classic **RAUNCHY**, which climbed to second place in the USA charts of 1957 (it made No. 11 over here the following year). It attracted a clutch of pale imitations at the time, generally much too sophisticated. In fact, RAUNCHY

---

33 The song was most closely associated of course with Marlene Dietrich (who joined the American war effort in 1941). Les Woosey offers a different perspective. "My childhood recollection is of Anne Shelton's words rather than those Americanised croakings of Dietrich. The two are quite different. Shelton was the first to sing and record Tommy Connor's English lyric (at Churchill's express request some say). ... Later on, the American OSS recruited the naturalised Dietrich to recreate the same miracle for the US forces ...".

34 An element prescribed by Joseph Goebbels' Propaganda Ministry! LILI MARLENE was actually based on a World War I poem by German soldier Hans Leip, subsequently set to music by Norbert Schultze (in 1938). Les Woosey again: "Real-life Danish cabaret actress and songstress Lale Anderson then recorded the song in German. It was the first German million-seller".

35 For those who cannot get enough of this piece, there are three versions from Tex Ritter, together with the Frankie Laine rendition, on the 2001 CD *High Noon: 25 Artists, One Song*, Bear Family BCD 16395 AR; more on this in *Record Collector* No. 263 (July 2001) 153.

owed its distinctiveness to the rough and ready production, and of course to that hooting sax (Justis) cum catchy guitar-riff (Manker). Not one of the best covers.

For the remaining six tracks of this survey we jump to the 1980s. First, **CHARIOTS OF FIRE**. One of the high points of synthesiser wizard Vangelis' distinguished career was the award of an Oscar in 1982 for Best Original Score in the previous year's acclaimed film of that name. The title track was a hit worldwide, making the top spot in the USA (in the UK it peaked at No. 12 the year before, though the soundtrack LP made fifth place). The Shadows naturally do not attempt to emulate the expansive soundstage and awesome grandeur of the original, but they do full justice in their own terms to this most potent of melodies, as at 1m 32s Hank's guitar dazzlingly takes over from Cliff Hall's majestic piano opening.

Vangelis went on to produce a number of impressive film scores (see on #14), one of which was commissioned for the 1982 political thriller 'Missing'. The captivating **THEME FROM MISSING** furnishes the kind of mellow, haunting melody that was tailor-made for Hank, who rises to the occasion, supported by an exceptionally well-judged accompaniment. Both this and CHARIOTS OF FIRE certainly do Vangelis proud.

Life In The Jungle has an immediate appeal to those Shadows' fans who do not care for "covers", since fifty per cent of the Album consists of brand new numbers. On this occasion, however, it is the reworked material that steals most of the limelight: the top-notch instrumentals HIGH NOON, THEME FROM MISSING, CHARIOTS OF FIRE, LILI MARLENE plus the vocal TREAT ME NICE set against the better of the originals, NO DANCING!, THE OLD ROMANTICS together with Martin Jenner's RIDERS OF THE RANGE. There was also a free LP thrown in (see on #15), so it seems churlish to suggest that the studio Album might have offered another couple of tracks to bring it into line in terms of duration with *Hits Right Up Your Street.*

Originals Of Cover Versions

• HIGH NOON
UK Single:
Frankie Laine, Columbia DB 3113 (1952)
CD:
See main text above

• **THEME FROM MISSING**
CD:
Vangelis, *Themes*,
Polydor 839518–2,
track 2 (1989)

• **TREAT ME NICE**
UK Single:
(A-side: 'Jailhouse Rock') Elvis Presley, RCA 1028 (1958)
CD:
Elvis' Golden Records, RCA 07863 / 67462 2, track 12 (1997)

• **CHARIOTS OF FIRE**
UK Single:
Vangelis, Polydor POSP 246 (1981/82)
CD:
As above, track 14

• **LILI MARLENE**
CD:
Lili Marlene — The Best Of Marlene Dietrich, Spectrum 544 293–2, track 9 (2000)
Also:
Lale Anderson:
40's Magic / 40's Dance Bands, Artistry LCE 973098 CD, track 6 (n.d.)
Anne Shelton:
Forces Sweethearts, ASV Living Era CD AJA 5260, track 18 (1999)

• **RAUNCHY**
UK Single:
Bill Justis, London HLS 8517 (1958)
CD:
Various Artists, *Teen Beat 4*, ACE CDCHD 655, track 8 (1997)

September 1982

#15

• LP, Polydor SHADS 1 ~ 2812 134:
Live At Abbey Road

Track Listing / Composers

1 THE THIRD MAN
Anton Karas
2 THING-ME-JIG
Hank Marvin / Bruce Welch / Brian Bennett
3 RUNAWAY
Del Shannon / Max Crook
4 ALL I HAVE TO DO IS DREAM
Boudleaux Bryant
5 IT DOESN'T MATTER ANY MORE
Paul Anka
6 JOHNNY B GOODE
Chuck Berry
7 OVER IN A FLASH
Hank Marvin / Alan Jones / Brian Bennett / Cliff Hall
8 SUMMER LOVE '59
Hank Marvin / Bruce Welch / Brian Bennett
9 OH BOY!
Sunny West / Norman Petty / Bill Tilghman
10 CRYING IN THE RAIN
Howard Greenfield / Carole King
11 ARTY'S PARTY
Hank Marvin / Bruce Welch / Brian Bennett

Vocal Tracks
3–6, 9–10

Distribution
UK only (see below)

CD Issues
See #53 and #93

Stage Performances

A number of the vocals featured on this LP were performed prior to 1982; thereafter, on the basis of the data assembled by George Geddes, *On Stage* pp. 9–12: in 1982/83 OH BOY!, in 1983 RUNAWAY, ALL I HAVE TO DO IS DREAM, in 1984 JOHNNY B GOODE.

****

A variation on the principle of "Buy One Get One Free" was dangled before purchasers of *Life In The Jungle*, since the Abbey Road set of live recordings from 2 July 1982[36] came with it, in the UK at any rate.

Tracks 1, 2, 8 and 11 were recent Polydor numbers already examined (see Index Of Titles). On this particular version of **THE THIRD MAN**, the ping of the lead guitar approximates more closely to Karas' original zither-tone; **ARTY'S PARTY** is used as a peg on which to hang an extended solo from Brian Bennett, close on 6 minutes long.

One fresh instrumental comes in the form of **OVER IN A FLASH**, an unpretentious piece of fun, very much a one-off: the sort of thing that might have been at home as background to one of Benny Hill's wordless sketches.

The remaining six tracks are of some historic importance: vocals which never made it on to record (legally anyway), representative of the kind of material worked into Shadows' tours of the late 70s/ early 80s.

A real curiosity among these is the 1961 UK/ USA Number One, Del Shannon's **RUNAWAY**. This is taken at a *very* relaxed pace: excellent harmonies and a fine Mark Knopfleresque guitar solo, but it is questionable whether this angst-ridden classic should be accorded such treatment. Certainly there is not a shred of the unrelieved "misery" so central to the song: bathos rather than pathos?

---

36 Further details on the goings-on here can be found in the sleevenotes (by Rob Bradford and David Martin) to the CD *Live At Abbey Road / Live At The Liverpool Empire* (#93 below).

Much more satisfying is **ALL I HAVE TO DO IS DREAM**, one of a host of covers of the great Everly Brothers' effortlessly smooth Number One either side of the water in 1958; the combination of guitar and keyboards is especially effective on this track. A less successful release (No. 6 both here and there in 1962) from the selfsame duo was **CRYING IN THE RAIN**, lovingly recreated here.

Another chart-topper (here in 1959, though not in the USA) was Buddy Holly's posthumously released **IT DOESN'T MATTER ANY MORE**: the kind of number to which Marvin Welch & Farrar (shades of them here) might have done full justice had they been in the habit of recording other composers' works.

The Shadows had issued an instrumental version of the stupendous (and much imitated) **JOHNNY B GOODE** (a 1958 Number Eight hit for Chuck Berry in the USA) on the underrated 1970 LP *Shades Of Rock*. The vocal rendition offered here demonstrates that The Shadows always were a great rock band: spirited solo spots from both Hank Marvin and Cliff Hall.

Another constantly recycled song, The Crickets' (with Buddy Holly on vocals) **OH BOY!** (a Number Three in February 1958) is put through its paces here, with an imaginative guitar solo thrown in.

Originals Of Cover Versions

• RUNAWAY
UK Single:
Del Shannon, London HLX 9317 (1961)
CD:
Runaway With Del Shannon / Hats Off To Del Shannon, BGO BGOCD 367, track 15 (1997)

• ALL I HAVE TO DO IS DREAM
UK Single:
The Everly Brothers, London HLA 8618 (1958)
CD:
The Definitive Everly Brothers, WSM 0927 47304–2, Disc 1/5 (2002)

• IT DOESN'T MATTER ANY MORE
UK Single:
Buddy Holly, Coral Q 72360 (1959)
CD:
The Very Best Of Buddy Holly And The Crickets, Universal Music TV 112 046–2, track 15 (1999)

• JOHNNY B GOODE
US Single:
Chuck Berry, Chess 1691 (1958)
CD:
The Best Of Chuck Berry, MCA MCD 11560, Disc 1/3 (1996)

• OH BOY!
UK Single:
The Crickets, Coral Q 72298 (1957)
CD:
As for Buddy Holly above, track 4

• CRYING IN THE RAIN
UK Single:
The Everly Brothers, Warner Bros WB 56 (1962)
CD:
As above, Disc 2/1

1982

#16

• Overseas Single, Polydor 2059 581:
CHARIOTS OF FIRE / LIFE IN THE JUNGLE

Issued in Finland; both tracks taken from *Life In The Jungle* (#14).

1982

#17

• Overseas LP, Polydor 6878 126:
Space Hits

WE DON'T TALK ANYMORE / ONE DAY I'LL FLY AWAY / THE THIRD MAN / SAILING / THE WINNER TAKES IT ALL / IMAGINE : WOMAN / MISTY / IF YOU LEAVE ME NOW* / CHI MAI / THIS OLE HOUSE / EQUINOXE (PART V)* / ALBATROSS* / TELSTAR / MORE THAN I CAN SAY / ARTY'S PARTY* / JUST THE WAY YOU ARE*

Issued in Holland; TV-promoted, it entered the Dutch charts on 27 February 1982, where it stayed for 9 weeks, peaking at No. 11 (information kindly supplied by Harry de Louw). This ineptly-titled 16–tracker was the first Polydor Shadows compilation LP: five tracks from *Change Of Address* (#2, asterisked above), the remainder from *Hits Right Up Your Street* (#8). Both Albums had been released in their own right in Holland. — Only one group original, ARTY'S PARTY.

1983

August 1983

#18

• Single, Polydor POSP 629 ~ 815 343–7:
DIAMONDS / ELEVENIS

Composers
Side A: Jerry Lordan
Side B: Bruce Welch / Hank Marvin / Brian Bennett

Top 20 Placing, *SCOFA* Poll (Polydor) 1992
No. 11= ELEVENIS

Top 20 Placing, Best Instro 1970–1990, *Shadsfax* Poll (Polydor +) 2001
No. 14 ELEVENIS

Distribution
UK only [2 different labels]

First Appearance On CD
Side A: *XXV* (UK 1987) 6 (#41)
Side B: *Dancing In The Dark* (UK 1990/91) 14 (#62/ #64)

On DIAMONDS see #19. The superlative B-side ("If TENNIS why not ELEVENIS?" seems to be the proposition underlying the wacky title[37]) more than compensates for the lacklustre cover version. Stylistically, it would have been pretty much at home on the *Tasty* LP of 1977.

August 1983 [+ Reissue??[38]]

#19

• 2 LP, Tellydisc Telly 22:
The Shadows' Silver Album

* = Wholly new tracks; for explanation of symbols A–C see main text below

[37] A more recherché explanation with reference to accomplished punster Victor Borge is suggested in *SCOFA* 5 (1983) 16.
[38] So Cortada and Broche. I cannot verify this.

Record 1

<THEME FROM THE DEER HUNTER: EMI> / MOZART FORTE[A] / CHI MAI[B] / <CLASSICAL GAS: EMI> / CHARIOTS OF FIRE[C] / <DON'T CRY FOR ME ARGENTINA: EMI> // MEMORY* / JUST THE WAY YOU ARE[A] / UP WHERE WE BELONG* / THE THIRD MAN[B] / YOU DON'T HAVE TO SAY YOU LOVE ME* / EQUINOXE (PART V)[A]

Record 2

SHADOOGIE '83* / QUEEN OF HEARTS* / <WALK DON'T RUN: EMI> / HATS OFF TO WALLY[B] / DIAMONDS* / TIME IS TIGHT* // ALBATROSS[A] / ONE DAY I'LL FLY AWAY[B] / GOING HOME* / AFRICA* / A WHITER SHADE OF PALE* / IF YOU LEAVE ME NOW[A] / IMAGINE : WOMAN[B]

Composers (New tracks)

• MEMORY
Andrew Lloyd Webber [lyrics: T S Eliot ~ Trevor Nunn]
• UP WHERE WE BELONG
Will Jennings / Buffy Saint-Marie / Jack Nitzsche
• YOU DON'T HAVE TO SAY YOU LOVE ME
Pino Donaggio / Vito Pallavicini
• SHADOOGIE '83
Hank Marvin / Bruce Welch / Jet Harris / Tony Meehan
• QUEEN OF HEARTS
Hank De Vito
• DIAMONDS
Jerry Lordan
• TIME IS TIGHT
Booker T Jones
• GOING HOME
Mark Knopfler
• AFRICA
David Paich / Jeff Porcaro
• A WHITER SHADE OF PALE
Keith Reid / Gary Brooker

Vocal Tracks

None

Top 20 Placing, *SCOFA* Poll (Polydor +) 1985

No. 4	TIME IS TIGHT
No. 6	MEMORY
No. 9	GOING HOME
No. 13	AFRICA

Top 20 Placing, *SCOFA* Poll (Polydor) 1992

No. 3	GOING HOME
No. 11=	MEMORY
No. 17	TIME IS TIGHT

Top 20 Placing, Best Cover, *Shadsfax* Poll (Polydor +) 2001

No. 2	GOING HOME
No. 11	TIME IS TIGHT
No. 14	QUEEN OF HEARTS

Top 20 Placing, Best Instro 1970–1990, *Shadsfax* Poll (Polydor +) 2001

No. 9	GOING HOME

Distribution

UK only (TV advertised, sold via mail-order; so not eligible for chart-placing)

Associated Singles (New tracks)

A-side	
DIAMONDS	#18
GOING HOME	#22
B-side	
GOING HOME	#46

CD Issue

None

First Appearance On CD

• *Compact Shadows* (UK 1984, #26)
MEMORY (track 4), QUEEN OF HEARTS (13), GOING HOME (18), AFRICA (6)
• *Moonlight Shadows* (UK 1986, #36)
A WHITER SHADE OF PALE (track 8)
• *XXV* (UK 1987, #41)
UP WHERE WE BELONG (track 3), YOU DON'T HAVE TO SAY YOU LOVE ME (4), DIAMONDS (6), TIME IS TIGHT (7)
• *The Shadows: Complete* (UK 1992, #70)
SHADOOGIE '83 (Disc 1/2)

Stage Performances

On the basis of the data assembled by George Geddes, *On Stage* pp. 10–12, both SHADOOGIE and TIME IS TIGHT were recurrent through the rest of the 80s[39]; also performed were MEMORY (1983/84/85) and GOING HOME (1983).

All that EMI contributed to the celebration of The Shadows' 25 years in showbusiness was a clutch of four tracks on this heavily advertised mail-order only 2LP set.[40] In addition, there were five tracks from *Change Of Address* (= A in the track listing above), five from *Hits Right Up Your Street* (= B), with only CHARIOTS OF FIRE from *Life In The Jungle* (= C). Among these, room was found for only one pure group original, HATS OFF TO WALLY, sourced from the second of the above Albums. So the public was hardly offered a profile of The Shadows as they really were.

The residual ten tracks were new, though one of them, DIAMONDS, had been issued shortly before on a Single, see #18. Here again there was only one group composition, an updated version of **SHADOOGIE**: performed with verve and dexterity, but rather colourless — lacking the magic of that glorious opening track on the first LP back in 1961. The same might be said, with greater force, of the elaborate (arguably overelaborate, with too much competing for the listener's attention) rendition of **DIAMONDS** in comparison with the thrusting Jet Harris / Tony Meehan Number One Single of 1963 (it deposed The Shadows' DANCE ON!).

Of the eight other covers, three were derived from high performers in the 1960s. As Dave Dee colourfully remarked of Dusty Springfield's **YOU DON'T HAVE TO SAY YOU LOVE ME** (March 1966 *Melody Maker*): "... a big hit. I've got shivers up and down my spine." He was right, as this poignant (originally Italian) love-song gave Dusty a UK Number One that year (and it was her biggest Stateside hit, before she teamed up with The Pet Shop Boys, that is). Thanks to Hank's sweetly singing lead, and the carefully crafted accompaniment, this is one of The Shadows' finest ballad instros.[41]

A second UK chart-topper represented here was one that came the way of Procol Harum in 1967. **A WHITER SHADE OF PALE** without those distinctive

---

[39] Both also in 1990: see the reports in *SCOFA* 25 (1990) 4 and 26 (1991) 14–15.
[40] Nonetheless, it "went on to sell 300,000 copies", *Bruce Welch, Rock 'n' Roll — I Gave You The Best Years Of My Life* (Viking: London 1989) 212.
[41] It is singled out for particular praise by Philip King in *SCOFA* 18 (1988) 18.

surreal lyrics? Well, the melody, heavily influenced by J S Bach[42], was a potent one, and The Shadows give a sensitive, beautifully scored account of one of the decade's great classics.

Lastly for this decade we trade one instrumental for another. Booker T and The MGs' superlative **TIME IS TIGHT**, from Booker T's score for the movie 'Up Tight', made No. 4 in 1969 (their biggest hit in this country). It is the kind of effortlessly flowing number that suited The Shadows down to the ground — and they do it proud.[43]

A solitary representative of the following decade is a purely instrumental version of Dave Edmunds' **QUEEN OF HEARTS**, one of a number of fine tracks on his splendid Album *Repeat Where Necessary* and a No. 11 in the Singles charts of 1979. As the arrangement of the original is followed closely, Bruce Welch's rhythm guitar, often barely noticeable, if at all, in recordings of the 80s, is strongly in evidence. An excellent choice.

Covers — all instrumental — of four hits from the 1980s complete the collection.

In 1981 Elaine Paige only took **MEMORY** from 'Cats' to No. 6 (the soundtrack Album peaked at No. 6 also), but, as the rash of cover versions has since shown, it has proved to be one of Andrew Lloyd Webber's most enduring creations. Needless to say, The Shadows' rendition is a masterly reflection of the song's exquisite beauty and poise. An equally satisfying inclusion is an authoritative version of a piece comparable in terms of chart performance (reaching No. 7 here in 1983, but a Number One in the USA the year before), **UP WHERE WE BELONG**, a moving love song commissioned for the end-titles of the movie 'An Officer And A Gentleman', performed by Joe Cocker and Jennifer Warnes.

Another Number One over there but not over here (where it made No. 3), in 1983, was the highly imaginative **AFRICA**, derived from the Album *Toto IV*, which went on to scoop up six Grammy Awards. The Shadows turn it into a sparkling instrumental, with that famous ringing Fender fully to the fore. An ideal opening track, as the compiler of *XXV* saw (#21), and one of the very best covers of the 80s.

---

[42] *Orchestral Suite No. 3 in D*, BWV 1068.
[43] For a description of the number, and its special place in the group's stage act, see Rob Bradford, sleevenotes to 1998 CD *Guardian Angel ... Plus*.

Lastly, **GOING HOME**: Mark Knopfler's theme from the movie 'Local Hero' stalled at No. 56 in the UK charts of 1983, but the soundtrack Album did considerably better with a No. 14. Hank Marvin's majestic guitar figures and Cliff Hall's stylish accompaniment combine to make the final track of this review one of the most radiant of the many covers attempted by the group — not as flamboyant as the original certainly, but none the worse for that. For an edited version see on #22.

To reiterate a point made at the start, as an anniversary collection this set scarcely begins to do justice to The Shadows' varied output, or to their own considerable gifts as composers. Still, the brand new covers taken together are pretty impressive; and, with the exception of the rejigged SHADOOGIE, they are all to be found on the Album which is the subject of the next entry but one, *XXV*.[44]

Originals Of Cover Versions

• MEMORY
UK Single:
Elaine Paige, Polydor POSP 279 (1981/82)
CD:
On Reflection: The Very Best Of Elaine Paige, Telstar TV ITVCD 2999, track 1 (1998)

• UP WHERE WE BELONG
UK Single:
Joe Cocker and Jennifer Warnes, Island WIP 6830 (1983)
CD:
The Best Of Joe Cocker, Capitol 0777 7 80512 2 0, track 4 (1992)

[44] I am in agreement here with Rob Bradford, who comments on *XXV*: "Excellent arrangements and passionate playing" (*Pipeline* 43 [1999] 38).

• YOU DON'T HAVE TO SAY YOU LOVE ME
UK Single:
Dusty Springfield, Philips BF 1482 (1966)
CD:
Dusty: The Very Best Of Dusty Springfield, Mercury/ Philips 538 345–2, track 7 (1998)

• SHADOOGIE ('83)
LP track:
The Shadows,
Columbia 33 SX 1374/ SCX 3414, track 1 (1961)
CD:
The Original Chart Hits 1960–1980,
EMI CD 7937522,
Disc 1/10 (1990)

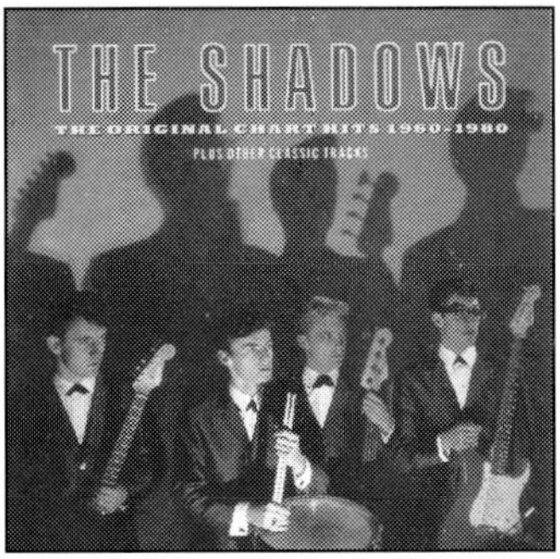

• QUEEN OF HEARTS
UK Single:
Dave Edmunds, Swansong SSK 19419 (1979)
CD:
The Dave Edmunds Anthology (1968–1990), Rhino R2 71191, Disc 2/4 (1993)

• DIAMONDS
UK Single:
Jet Harris and Tony Meehan,
Decca F 11563 (1963)
CD:
The Best Of Jet Harris & Tony Meehan,
Spectrum 544 268–2,
track 1 (2000)

• TIME IS TIGHT
UK Single:
Booker T and The MGs, Stax 119 (1969)
CD:
The Best Of Booker T & The MGs, Ace CDSXK–123, track 5 (1998)

• GOING HOME
UK Single:
Mark Knopfler,
Vertigo/ Phonogram DSTR 4 (1983)
CD:
Screenplaying,
Vertigo 518 327–2,
track 18 (1993)

• AFRICA
UK Single:
Toto,
CBS A 2510 (1983)
CD:
Past To Present: 1977–1990,
Columbia 4659982,
track 2 (1990)

• A WHITER SHADE OF PALE
UK Single:
Procol Harum, Deram DM 126 (1967)
CD:
Greatest Hits, Metro METRCD038, track 1 (2000)

August 1983

#20

• LP, Polydor SPELP 8:
Change Of Address

UK budget reissue of #2, q.v.

October 1983

#21

• LP, Polydor POLD 5120:
XXV

AFRICA / GOING HOME / UP WHERE WE BELONG / YOU DON'T HAVE TO SAY YOU LOVE ME / THE MODERN WAY // DIAMONDS / TIME IS TIGHT / MEMORY / LIVERPOOL DAYS / QUEEN OF HEARTS / A WHITER SHADE OF PALE

Composers (New tracks)
• THE MODERN WAY
Harry Bogdanovs
• LIVERPOOL DAYS
Anthony Catchpole / Ron Roker / Winston Sela

Vocal Tracks
The two above

UK Chart Performance

Date of first chart entry:	22 October 1983
Highest position in chart:	*34*
Weeks in chart:	6

Top 20 Placing, *SCOFA* Poll (Polydor +) 1985
No. 18 LIVERPOOL DAYS

Distribution
UK, and Australia, France, Holland, Japan, New Zealand, Portugal, Spain — For a South African release see #29

CD Issue
See #41 (first appearance on CD for tracks 5, 9)

****

In the footsteps of the Tellydisc *Silver Album* (#19) along came Polydor with *XXV* — not a fresh celebratory set, but a second helping of no less than nine of the eleven tracks from the mail-order LPs, SHADOOGIE '83 falling by the wayside, with only DIAMONDS to represent a firm if indirect link with The Shadows' past.

The two novelties, both vocals:
THE MODERN WAY is an ambitious, showy song, clocking in at over 6m, with Hank on lead vocal passionately deploring the ways of the 80s, and the composer contributing a robust, at times florid, keyboard accompaniment; Bogdanovs was formerly a member of the group Astra, and went on to work with Kiki Dee, Elton John, David Knopfler and others.
The sentimentality of **LIVERPOOL DAYS**, for this writer at least, who lived through the period in question, is just too cloying for comfort. Totally outclassed by the tracks either side of it.

December 1983

#22

• Single, Polydor POSP 657 ~ 8159 37–7[45]:
GOING HOME / CAT 'N' MOUSE
•• Promo Single Polydor PODJ 657 has edited version of GOING HOME

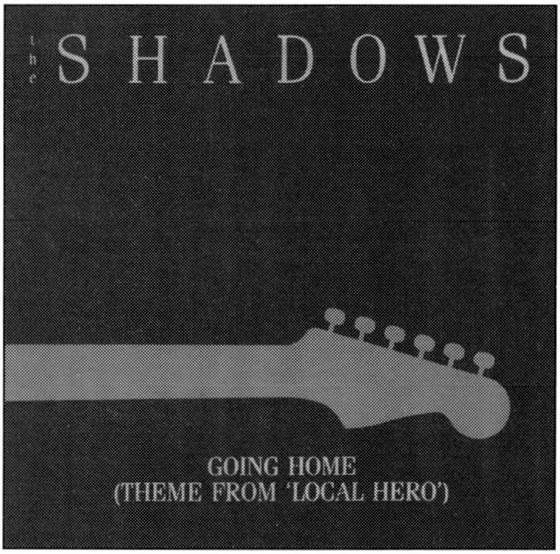

Composers

Side A Mark Knopfler
Side B Bruce Welch / Hank Marvin / Brian Bennett

Distribution

UK only [2 different labels]

Overseas Variation

#46 THEMES FROM EASTENDERS & HOWARD'S WAY / GOING HOME

First Appearance On CD

Side A *Compact Shadows* (UK 1984) 18 (#26); [edit] *Shadows In The Night* (UK 1993) 13 (#71)
Side B *Life In The Jungle* (UK 1989) 5 (#52)

[45] And not, as one would expect, 815 937–7.

For GOING HOME, from *The Shadows' Silver Album*, see on #19. On the DJ edit, the introduction (though in its full form not nearly as long as that of the original Knopfler version) is shortened by some 20s. CAT 'N' MOUSE is from *Life In The Jungle*, see on #14.

1983

#23

• Overseas LP, EMI HMVNZ 23:
20 Golden Greats Vol. 2

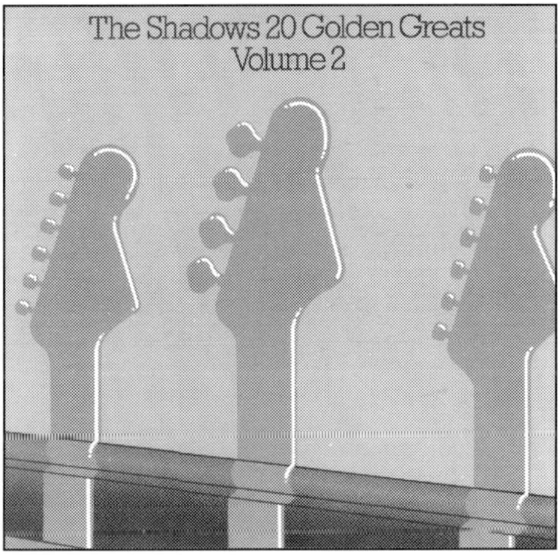

* = Polydor tracks

THEME FROM THE DEER HUNTER / SHADOOGIE† / SACHA [Hank Marvin] / TALES OF A RAGGY TRAMLINE / PEACE PIPE / SHAZAM! / 36–24–36 / ALBATROSS* / RHYTHM AND GREENS / BRIGHT EYES // THIS OLE HOUSE* / THE THIRD MAN* / QUATERMASSTER'S STORES / THE BOYS / TELSTAR* / CHI MAI* / CLASSICAL GAS / CHARIOTS OF FIRE* / DON'T CRY FOR ME ARGENTINA / THEME FROM MISSING*

† Record re-pressed; on original pressing SHADOOGIE was supplanted by NIVRAM

Vocal Tracks
None

****

Issued in New Zealand — Australasia's first go at a blend of EMI + Roll Over product is a bit of a hotch-potch. Representing Polydor UK we get ALBATROSS from *Change Of Address* (#2); THIS OLE HOUSE, THE THIRD MAN, TELSTAR and CHI MAI from *Hits Right Up Your Street* (#8); CHARIOTS OF FIRE and THEME FROM MISSING from *Life In The Jungle* (#14). No group compositions here; the emphasis is very much on covers of instrumentals.

See also #75 below (CD derivative).

1984

August 1984

#24

• Single, Polydor POSP 694 ~ 881 159–7:
ON A NIGHT LIKE THIS / THING-ME-JIG

Composers
Side A John David
Side B Hank Marvin / Bruce Welch / Brian Bennett

Distribution
UK [2 different labels], and Bolivia [33 rpm???], New Zealand

First Appearance On CD
Side A *Guardian Angel* (UK 1984) 9 (#27); see also on #91!
Side B *Compact Shadows* (UK 1984) 7 (#26)

This country-rock A-side, to be found on the Album *Guardian Angel* (see above), was produced by Stuart Coleman, who set Shakin' Stevens on the road to chart success when he became his producer in 1980[46]; composer John David was responsible for some of Stevens' songs. This was the second — and the last — Polydor vocal Single track.

For the older THING-ME-JIG see on #8.

August 1984

#25

• LP, Polydor SPELP 78:
Hits Right Up Your Street

UK budget reissue of #8, q.v.

Hull 1984
Photograph: John Hank Humphrey

[46] Coleman had also produced the Cliff Richard/ Phil Everly 'She Means Nothing To Me' in October 1982.

September 1984

#26

• CD, Polydor 823 080–2:

Compact Shadows

EQUINOXE (PART V)[A] / THE THIRD MAN[B] / NO DANCING![C/*] / MEMORY[D] / CHI MAI[B] / AFRICA[D] / THING-ME-JIG[B/*] / THEME FROM MISSING[C] / MOZART FORTE[A] / IF YOU LEAVE ME NOW[A] / SUMMER LOVE '59[B/*] / HELLO MR W.A.M.[A] / QUEEN OF HEARTS[D] / MORE THAN I CAN SAY[B] / LIFE IN THE JUNGLE[C/*] / CHARIOTS OF FIRE[C] / SAILING[B] / GOING HOME[D]

Running Time
70m 15s

Vocal Tracks
None

Distribution
UK, and Germany, Japan, Korea

The first Shadows' CD[47]. An ample and varied set of 18 tracks, over 70m in duration[48], offering LP material from: *Change Of Address* (4, = A above), *Hits Right Up Your Street* (6, = B), *Life In The Jungle* (4, = C), *The Silver Album / XXV* (4, = D). Four original group compositions were included, asterisked in the track listing.

To enjoy a number of tracks in digital form, enthusiasts had to make do with this CD for some years to come: of the source Albums listed above, the CD counterparts appeared in 1992, 1987, 1989 and (*XXV*) 1987 respectively.

November 1984

#27

• LP/ CD, Polydor POLD 5169 ~ 823 797–1 // 823 797–2:
Guardian Angel

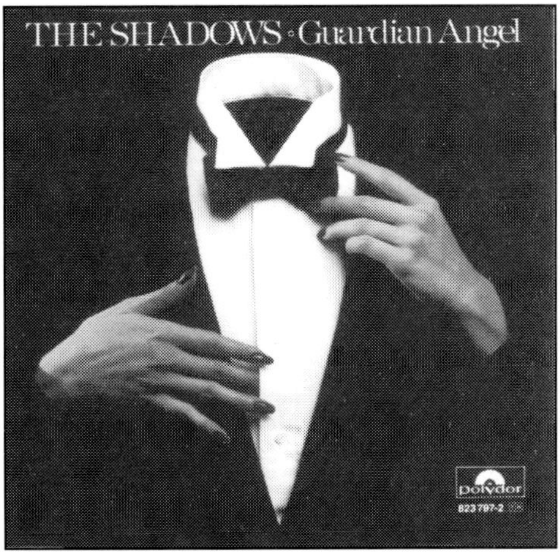

47 The first EMI Shadows' CD had to wait until 1986. EMI was very slow in taking up the new medium. One reason was that the company dithered for some while about the possible adoption of a rival contact (!) laser system from JVC (Victor Company of Japan) — an aspect lost sight of amid the general haze in the account of Peter Markland, *EMI — The First 100 Years* (Batsford: London 1997) 258.

48 More modestly, a flash on the front cover boasts "OVER 60 MINUTES OF MUSIC".

Track Listing / Composers

1 HOW DO I LOVE THEE
Eddie Phillips

2 HAMMERHEAD
Dick Plant

3 THE SATURDAY WESTERN
Tim Renwick

4 LOOK BACK ON LOVE
Brian Bennett

5 JOHNNY STACCATO
Hank Marvin / Bruce Welch / Brian Bennett

6 I WILL RETURN
Philip Cordell //

7 (I WANNA BE YOUR) GUARDIAN ANGEL
Kevin Fitzpatrick

8 CAN'T PLAY YOUR GAME
Keith Wilkinson / Anthony Wimshurst

9 ON A NIGHT LIKE THIS
John David

10 TURNING POINT
Hank Marvin / Bruce Welch / Brian Bennett

11 OUR ALBERT
Hank Marvin / Brian Bennett

Vocal Tracks

7–9

UK Chart Performance

Date of first chart entry:	17 November 1984
Position in chart (single week):	*98*

Top 20 Placing, *SCOFA* Poll (Polydor +) 1985

No. 3	HAMMERHEAD
No. 8	GUARDIAN ANGEL
No. 11	HOW DO I LOVE THEE
No. 17	JOHNNY STACCATO

Top 20 Placing, *SCOFA* Poll (Polydor) 1992

No. 5	HOW DO I LOVE THEE
No. 7	HAMMERHEAD
No. 13	GUARDIAN ANGEL
No. 14	THE SATURDAY WESTERN

Top 20 Placing, Best Instro 1970–1990, *Shadsfax* Poll (Polydor +) 2001

No. 8	HAMMERHEAD
No. 12	JOHNNY STACCATO
No. 18	I WILL RETURN

Distribution: LP

UK, and Australia, France, Germany (x 2), Holland, Japan, New Zealand, Portugal

Distribution: CD

UK, and Germany — See also under #81 below (augmented version)

Running Time: CD

43m 49s

Associated Singles

A-side	
ON A NIGHT LIKE THIS	#24
HOW DO I LOVE THEE	#31
HAMMERHEAD	#32
A-side Promo	
GUARDIAN ANGEL	#28
B-side	
JOHNNY STACCATO	#31, #35
CAN'T PLAY YOUR GAME	#32
TURNING POINT	#37
B-side Promo	
HAMMERHEAD	#28
Track 3 on 12" // CD Single	
TURNING POINT	#38 // #50

Stage Performances

On the basis of the data assembled by George Geddes, *On Stage* pp. 11–12, only two numbers are in question, both from 1985 (Australia): HOW DO I LOVE THEE and HAMMERHEAD [see #31 and esp. #32].

Neither *Life In The Jungle* (#14) nor, for that matter, *Change Of Address* (#2) was exactly chock-full of chart covers, but *Guardian Angel* is freest of all of what many have come to regard as the bane of 1980's Shadows' Albums. The only commercially successful piece included is the anthemic **I WILL RETURN** by Springwater (= multi-instrumentalist Phil Cordell), Polydor 2058 141[49] (1971, peaking at No. 5) — a stirring piece more likely perhaps to appeal to Shadows stalwarts nurtured North of the Border! The original is followed pretty closely, though the instrumentation is more refined and incisive.

There is no need to provide a track-by-track analysis of this Album[50] since it has been described in great detail (and in glowing terms) by Rob Bradford in the sleevenotes to the 1998 CD *Guardian Angel ... Plus* (see #81). Given the author's well documented views on 80's cover versions though, I have to say that I do not sympathise with the implication that the one species of Album is without blemish, the other thoroughly flawed, indeed rather disreputable. The latter category will be looked at in due course. On the Album under present scrutiny, tracks 1, 2 and 6 ("bought in" material) and tracks 10 and 11 (original compositions) are especially fine. On the other hand: **THE SATURDAY WESTERN** strikes me as thoroughly lacklustre, resembling many of the pedestrian numbers on offer from the seemingly unending stream of Shads imitators: give me MUSTANG and the rest[51] any day! Also, I wonder whether I can be alone in finding the lyrics of **GUARDIAN ANGEL**, which veer between puerility and incoherence, riddled with an insufferable air of self-importance: is this guy really serious?[52] Still, the excellence of the remaining two vocal tracks[53] more than compensate for this dismal offering. Again, I am not persuaded that the complex **LOOK BACK ON LOVE**, naturally pulled out of its context, is entirely at home on a Shadows' Album: it is Library Music, though admittedly high grade Library Music.

The position of *Guardian Angel* among the group's Polydor Albums is discussed further in the Introduction.

---

49 CD: *Springwater*, Angel Air SJPCD 105, track 1 (2002).
50 Voted "Best Album 1980–1990" in Shadsfax Poll 2001, see *Shadsfax* 35 [2002] 16.
51 Or, from the Polydor era, RIDERS OF THE RANGE and HIGH NOON.
52 Admirers of the song can read composer Kevin Fitzpatrick's story in *Shadsfax* 24 (1999) 19–20.
53 Is I CAN'T PLAY YOUR GAME a "straightforward 'pop' song" (Rob Bradford)? It sounds pretty unusual and adventurous to me. Can Hank's striking accompaniment be paralleled in any of his other recordings?

1984

#28

• Overseas Promo Single, Polydor 881 509–7:
GUARDIAN ANGEL / HAMMERHEAD

Issued in France. See #27.

1984

#29

• Overseas 2LP, EMI EMCJ(E) + EMCJ(F) 5333:
XXV + The Shadows

A double-pack from South Africa. For *XXV* see #21; for the contents of *The Shadows* see *The Shadows At EMI* 426.

Hull 1984
Photograph: John Hank Humphrey

Hull 1984
Photographs: John Hank Humphrey

Hull 1984
Photoograph: John Hank Humphrey

Hull 1984
Photographs: John Hank Humphrey

1985

January 1985

#30

• LP, Polydor 2478 163 ~ SPELP 88:
Life In The Jungle

UK budget reissue of 1982 Album, see #14 (with all references to free Album removed!).

1985

#31

• Overseas Single, EMI 939:
HOW DO I LOVE THEE / JOHNNY STACCATO

Issued in New Zealand; both sides from LP *Guardian Angel* (#27).

1985

#32

• Overseas Single, EMI 1457:
HAMMERHEAD / CAN'T PLAY YOUR GAME

Issued in Australia; both sides from LP *Guardian Angel* (#27).

1985

#33

• Overseas LP, EMI Sound Value AXIS 169:
More Rarities

* = Polydor tracks

SPOT THE BALL* / RIDERS IN THE SKY / RUN BILLY RUN / IT'LL BE ME BABE / SWEET SATURDAY NIGHT / THE SHADY LADY* / THE FOURTH MAN* / LONDONDERRY AIR / KIMI TO ITSUMADEMO // RUSK / FENDER BENDER* / LOVE DELUXE / CRICKET BAT BOOGIE / SHADOOGIE '83* / OMOIDE NO NAGISA / GIN-IRO NO MICHI / BLACK IS BLACK / ELEVENIS*

****

Issued in New Zealand, this LP conveniently gathered together elusive B-sides of Polydor UK Singles: the first (#1), third (#6), sixth (#12), seventh (#13) and eighth (#18), adding for good measure the revamped SHADOOGIE which had appeared on *The Silver Album* (#19) but not on *XXV* (#21). (The selection of earlier, (UK) EMI tracks is not quite as satisfactory, see Ian Kershaw in *SCOFA* 17 [1988] 20.)

1985

#34

• Overseas 2LP, J & B Records JB 208–1/2:
Sounds Of Today

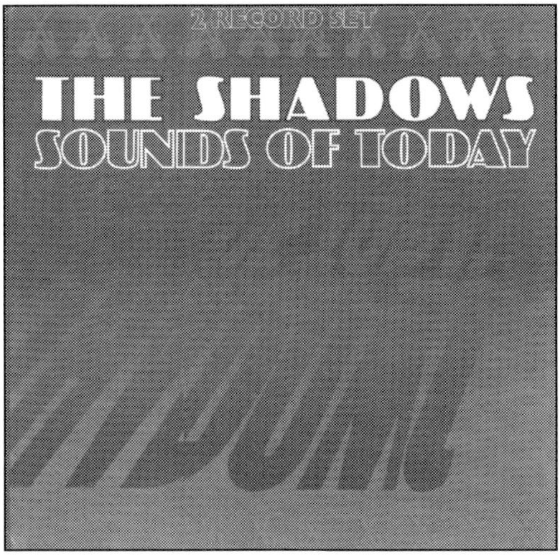

Record 1

GOING HOME / MEMORY / JUST THE WAY YOU ARE / UP WHERE WE BELONG / THE THIRD MAN / YOU DON'T HAVE TO SAY YOU LOVE ME / EQUINOXE (PART V) // SHADOOGIE '83 / QUEEN OF HEARTS / WALK DON'T RUN [EMI] / HATS OFF TO WALLY / DIAMONDS / TIME IS TIGHT

Record 2

THEME FROM THE DEER HUNTER [EMI] / MOZART FORTE / CHI MAI / / CLASSICAL GAS [EMI] / CHARIOTS OF FIRE / DON'T CRY FOR ME ARGENTINA [EMI] // ALBATROSS / ONE DAY I'LL FLY AWAY / AFRICA / A WHITER SHADE OF PALE / IF YOU LEAVE ME NOW / IMAGINE : WOMAN

Issued in Australia. In turning his hand to Grieg's Piano Concerto, the inimitable Eric Morecambe contended that all the notes were there, though not necessarily in the right order. Similarly here J & B Records have moved around all the components of *The Shadows' Silver Album* from August 1983 (#19), though the end result is not nearly as amusing.

See the review in *SCOFA* 11 (1986) 9.

1986

April 1986

#35

• Single, Polydor POSP 792 ~ 885 013–7:
MOONLIGHT SHADOW / JOHNNY STACCATO

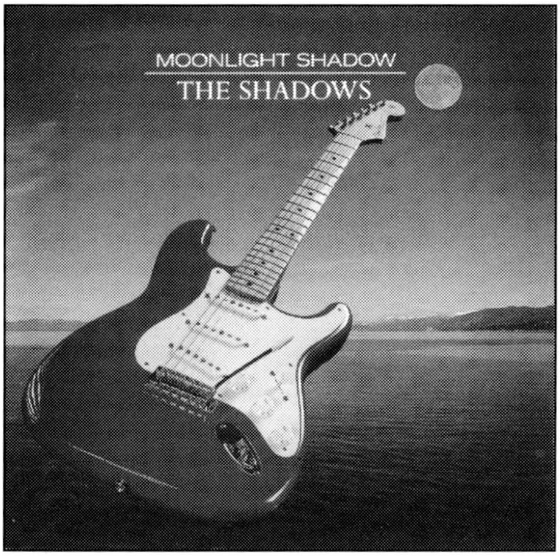

Composers
Side A: Mike Oldfield
Side B: Hank Marvin / Bruce Welch / Brian Bennett

Distribution
UK, and Germany, New Zealand

Overseas Variation
#31 HOW DO I LOVE THEE / JOHNNY STACCATO

First Appearance On CD

Side A: *Moonlight Shadows* (UK 1986) 9 (#36)
Side B: *Guardian Angel* (UK 1984) 5 (#27)

See #36 and #27. By the end of March 'Living Doll' from Cliff Richard & The Young Ones, with a guest appearance by Hank Marvin, had hit the top spot, but The Shadows simply continued on their chartless Singles path, despite the fact that MOONLIGHT SHADOW was given some TV exposure.

May 1986

#36

• LP/ CD, Polydor PROLP 8 ~ 829 358–1 // 829 358–2:
Moonlight Shadows

Track Listing / Composers

1 EVERY BREATH YOU TAKE
Sting

2 HELLO
Lionel Richie

3 THE POWER OF LOVE
Candy de Rouge / Gunther Mende / Jennifer Rush / Mary Susan Applegate

4 HEY JUDE
John Lennon / Paul McCartney
5 AGAINST ALL ODDS
Phil Collins
6 MEMORY
Andrew Lloyd Webber [lyrics T S Eliot / Trevor Nunn]
7 DANCING IN THE DARK
Bruce Springsteen
8 A WHITER SHADE OF PALE
Keith Reid / Gary Brooker //
9 MOONLIGHT SHADOW
Mike Oldfield
10 THREE TIMES A LADY
Lionel Richie
11 SAILING
Gavin Sutherland
12 I JUST CALLED TO SAY I LOVE YOU
Stevie Wonder
13 I KNOW HIM SO WELL
Benny Andersson / Tim Rice / Björn Ulvaeus
14 NIGHTS IN WHITE SATIN
Justin Hayward
15 IMAGINE : WOMAN
John Lennon
16 WALK OF LIFE
Mark Knopfler

Vocal Tracks
None

UK Chart Performance

Date of first chart entry:	24 May 1986
Highest position in chart:	*6*
Weeks in chart:	19

Top 20 Placing, *SCOFA* Poll (Polydor) 1992
No. 6 MOONLIGHT SHADOW
No. 18 NIGHTS IN WHITE SATIN

Top 20 Placing, Best Cover, *Shadsfax* Poll (Polydor +) 2001
No. 1 MOONLIGHT SHADOW

Top 20 Placing, Best Instro 1970–1990, *Shadsfax* Poll (Polydor +) 2001

No. 7 MOONLIGHT SHADOW
No. 19 DANCING IN THE DARK

Distribution: LP

UK, and Australia (x 2), Belgium/ Holland, France, Germany (x 2), Greece, Israel, New Zealand, Peru, Portugal — For a South African release see under #58.

Distribution: CD

UK (see also #77), and Australia[54], Germany, Japan, Korea, Malta, Mexico — For a retitled version issued in Australia see under #82 below.

Running Time: CD

66m 21s

Associated Singles

A-side	
MOONLIGHT SHADOW	#35
IMAGINE: WOMAN	#9
12" Single, 2nd track	
DANCING IN THE DARK	#38

Stage Performances

On the basis of the data assembled by George Geddes, *On Stage* p. 11, MOONLIGHT SHADOW was featured 1986/87; as also THREE TIMES A LADY (delivered as a vocal in 1978).

****

Over 66 minutes of Shadow music, but four of the sixteen tracks had appeared on previous Albums: SAILING and IMAGINE: WOMAN on *Hits Right Up Your Street* (#8), MEMORY and A WHITER SHADE OF PALE on *The Silver Album / XXV* (#19/ #21).

Taken overall, *Moonlight Shadows* differs from its Polydor predecessors in important respects:

---

54 A 1998 Karussel release founded on the annotated issue from Spectrum in 1996: see under #77.

• There are no group-originals, every track is a cover version.
• Not a single number started life as an instrumental.
• The emphasis is very much on recent releases: nine of the twelve fresh tracks recast chart material from the years 1983–1986, and high profile chart material at that: represented among the twelve are no less than five UK/USA Number Ones, two UK Number Ones, and one USA Number One.

First, two from the 1960s:
The Beatles' **HEY JUDE** was a chart-topper on either side of the Atlantic in 1968. This long distance composition, with Macca's soulful delivery, its distinctive "na, na, na, na-na-na-na" chorus, and the weighty 36-piece orchestral accompaniment, is so powerful and idiosyncratic that any imitation — vocal or otherwise — is bound to sound pale by comparison.[55] The Shadows demote HEY JUDE to the status of a catchy tune, overembellished in places.

Justin Hayward joined The Moody Blues in 1966: his **NIGHTS IN WHITE SATIN**, taken from the concept Album *Days Of Future Passed*, proved to have a recurrent impact on the UK charts, reaching No. 19 in 1967/68, No. 9 in 1972, and No. 14 in 1979, while in the USA it hit second place in 1972. Here was a truly big production piece, with the strings/ flutes etc. of The London Festival Orchestra joining forces with Hayward and the rest to provide an intensely dramatic but decidedly overblown sound-picture. The diminution in scale works to The Shadows' advantage: the emphasis is on the captivating melody, the grandeur of which is conveyed with both vigour and grace.

From one of Motown's prize acts of the 70s, The Commodores with lead vocalist Lionel Richie, came a love song with a ravishing melody which was tailor-made for the Marvin ballad technique. The award-winning **THREE TIMES A LADY** was an unsurprising chart-topper both in the USA and UK in 1978.

---

[55] All that I have heard anyway. An imposing, not to say overwhelming, collection of covers is assembled by Dave Henderson, *The Beatles Uncovered* (The Black Book Company Ltd: Pewsey 2000) 40. (If you actually want to track this little lot down, prepare yourself for some hard labour: no discographical data are given.)

The nine covers from the 1980s can be taken in the order in which they came to enjoy chart success:

•1983

It is hard to see how any fan of The Shadows could find fault with the rendition of **EVERY BREATH YOU TAKE**, which is a well-chosen opener for *Moonlight Shadows*. This was a multi-award-winning UK/USA Number One for The Police, and a standout track on their equally high-performing Album *Synchronicity*. The Shadows' version motors along authoritatively, conveying something of the insistent tone of Sting's theme of erotic obsessiveness. In my view one of the very best of the 80's tracks.

A further inventive Album from this same year, Mike Oldfield's *Crises*, featured the Number Four Single **MOONLIGHT SHADOW** (with vocals from the excellent Maggie Reilly). This provided The Shadows with another knockout track. The original was a dynamic production, with some pretty creditable guitar work from Mike Oldfield himself. Hank rises to the occasion with a magisterial performance, the highlight of which is a series of breathtaking runs from 2m 11s on.

• 1984

Two of the four tracks representing this year were taken from UK/USA Number Ones. Lionel Richie's sweet and sentimental ballad **HELLO** makes a fair instrumental, with a nimble-fingered solo-break from Hank at 2m 47s, and a fine accompaniment throughout. Another Single issued by Motown in similar vein, but with a stronger melody, was Stevie Wonder's **I JUST CALLED TO SAY I LOVE YOU**. The Shadows manage to capture much of the original's warmth, but, given its highly repetitive nature, their version, without the benefit of the impassioned vocals, surely outstays its welcome at over four and a quarter minutes; the attempt to provide a bit more diversity comes a bit late in the day , at 3m 30s.

A third song from 1984 was a chart-topper in the USA, and only narrowly missed the top in the UK (initially stopped in its tracks by Lionel Richie's HELLO). Phil Collins' Ivor Novello Award-winning **AGAINST ALL ODDS**, commissioned for the movie of the same name, elicits a sensitive performance from Hank Marvin, but the impact is blunted by failure to match the original's masterly exploitation of piano, percussion and swirling synths. Still, as with so many of the covers where the accompaniment leaves something to be desired, there is that incomparable guitar to consider ...

Finally for 1984, a version of the hard-edged rock star Bruce Springsteen's **DANCING IN THE DARK**, a Number Two in the USA; in the UK it reached only No. 28 (though the parent LP, *Born In The USA*, was a Number One in both countries), but when re-promoted in 1985, it made No. 4. A prominent feature of the number is the driving percussion, well reflected in The Shadows' rendition, and even more forcefully mirrored in the variants (see on #38).

•1985

Two very different Number Ones are represented here. Soaring vocals and powerful percussion combined on Jennifer Rush's **THE POWER OF LOVE** to produce a song of great emotional intensity. The Shadows' account is subdued (in places feeble) by comparison, and the outro seems over-extended.

More of the spirit of the model (with partial mimicking of the Abbaesque synths) is captured on **I KNOW HIM SO WELL**, from the musical 'Chess', an exquisite number performed to perfection by the formidably talented songstresses Elaine Paige and Barbara Dickson (even if they did not actually record the piece in each other's presence!). The *Moonlight* master tape evidently suffered a dropout at 03s, which ought to have been put right before release.

• 1986

WALK OF LIFE, which closes the Album, was one of a number of individual tracks marketed from the staggeringly successful Dire Straits' Album *Brothers In Arms*; this particular one made No. 2 in the UK and No. 7 in the USA. The impact of the song stems from its lyrics rather than its melodic content, and its credentials as an aspiring instrumental look distinctly umpromising. What lifts The Shadows' version is Hank's departure from the script into the realms of inventive improvising, without sacrificing the lightness of touch. Whatever verdict is passed on *Moonlight Shadows* as a whole, it must be owned that it ends with a real flourish.

Indeed, it seems a great pity that the more adventurous approach on this track, as on MOONLIGHT SHADOW, was not adopted more extensively. As it is, the inclusion of three or so group originals would have provided some diversification — but, as the back cover says, these are "Shadows unique interpretations of classic tracks"; and *Moonlight Shadows* took them to within shouting distance of the Top Five, as their most successful Polydor Album yet.

Originals Of Cover Versions

• EVERY BREATH YOU TAKE
UK Single:
The Police,
A & M AM 117 (1983)
CD:
The Very Best Of Sting And The Police,
A & M 493 252–2,
track 4 (2002)

• HELLO
UK Single:
Lionel Richie,
Motown TMG 1330 (1984)
CD:
Truly: The Love Songs,
Motown 530 843–2,
track 5 (1997)

• THE POWER OF LOVE
UK Single:
Jennifer Rush,
CBS A 5003 (1985)
CD:
Jennifer Rush,
Columbia 460947 2,
track 10 (1984)

• HEY JUDE
UK Single:
The Beatles, Apple R 5722 (1968)
CD:
1, EMI/ Apple 7243 5 299702 2, track 21 (2000)

• AGAINST ALL ODDS
UK Single:
Phil Collins,
Virgin VS 674 (1984)
CD:
Hits,
Virgin Records CDV 2870
~ 7243 8 46601 2 3,
track 7 (1998)

• DANCING IN THE DARK
UK Single:
Bruce Springsteen,
CBS A 4436 (1984/85)
CD:
Greatest Hits,
Columbia 478555 2,
track 7 (1995)

• MOONLIGHT SHADOW
UK Single:
Mike Oldfield,
Virgin VS 586 (1983)
CD:
The Best Of Mike Oldfield — Elements,
Virgin 7243 8 39069 2 5,
track 3 (1993)

• THREE TIMES A LADY
UK Single:
The Commodores, Motown TMG 1113 (1978)
CD:
Lionel Richie, *Truly* (as above), track 3

• I JUST CALLED TO SAY I LOVE YOU
UK Single:
Stevie Wonder,
Motown TMG 1349 (1984)
CD:
The Definitive Collection,
Universal 066–502–2,
Disc 1/6 (2002)

• I KNOW HIM SO WELL
UK Single:
Elaine Paige and Barbara Dickson,
RCA CHESS 3 (1985)
CD:
On Reflection: The Very Best Of Elaine Paige,
Telstar TV TTVCD 2999,
track 18 (1998)

• NIGHTS IN WHITE SATIN
UK Single:
The Moody Blues, Deram DM 161 (1967/1972/1979)
CD:
The Collection, Universal 560 241–2, Disc 1/3 (2001)

• WALK OF LIFE
UK Single:
Dire Straits,
Vertigo DSTR 12 (1986)
CD:
Brothers In Arms,
Vertigo 824499–2,
track 3 (1996)

September 1986

#37

• Single, Polydor POSP 808 ~ 885 162–7:
DANCING IN THE DARK (7" remix) / TURNING POINT

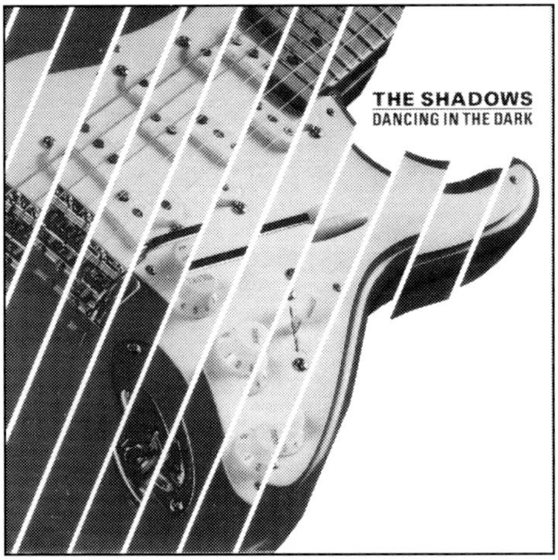

Composers

Side A: Bruce Springsteen
Side B: Hank Marvin / Bruce Welch / Brian Bennett

Distribution
UK, and New Zealand

First Appearance On CD
Side A: None: see next entry!
Side B: *Guardian Angel* (UK 1984) 10 (#27)

For the B-side see on #27.

September 1986

#38

• 12" Single, Polydor POSP X 808:
DANCING IN THE DARK (12" remix) /
DANCING IN THE DARK (Album* version) / TURNING POINT

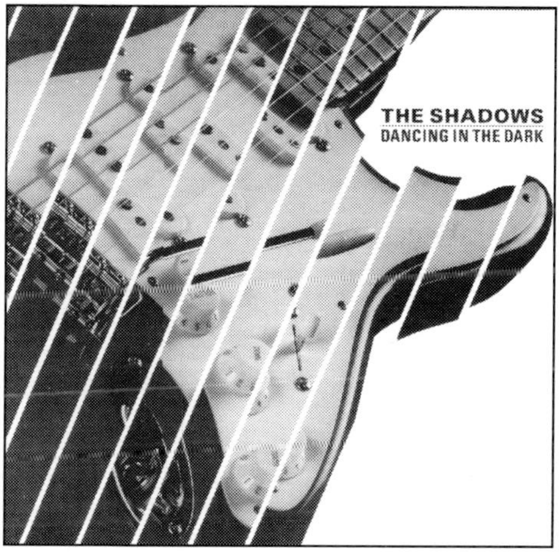

* Mistakenly listed as 7" version [see previous entry]

Distribution
UK, and New Zealand

First Appearance On CD [Track 1]
Guardian Angel ... Plus (UK 1998) 12 (#81)

The special remix of DANCING IN THE DARK was prepared for this, The Shadows' first, and only, 12" release[56], by Murray Munro: compared with the Album version (#36), the intro is much longer (close on 2m) and sprouts an infectious dance rhythm from 35s on; Hank's lead is subsequently supported by hard-edged synths and percussion; the whole track lasts 5m 30s as opposed to 3m 44s. What a pity more 80's Shadstrax were not accorded such treatment: the later SHADOWMIX (#55) was much less impressive.

The 7" remix (see previous entry) has close affinities with the 12", but it is much simplified, with a shrunken intro; and shorter than the Album version at 3m 33s. There is as yet no representation of the 7" on CD: although meant to be included on the 2001 CD *The Singles Collection*, astonishingly a variant version turned up instead: see on #91 below.

Brighton 1986
Photograph: John Hank Humphrey

[56] It is now seldom seen: "Some say that there are less than 1000 copies of the 12" single in circulation" remarks Jim Nugent, *Pipeline* 44 (1999) 57.

December 1986

#39

• Single, Polydor POSP 847 ~ 885 514–7:
THEMES FROM EASTENDERS AND HOWARD'S WAY / NO DANCING!

Composers
Side A: Simon May / Leslie Osborne
Side B: Bruce Welch / Hank Marvin / Brian Bennett

Distribution
UK, and Holland

Overseas Variation
#46 THEMES FROM ... / GOING HOME

First Appearance On CD
Side A: *Simply ... Shadows* (UK 1987) 12 (#44)
Side B: *Life In The Jungle* (UK 1989) 7 (#52)

See on #44 and #14. "This release was out in a hurry, immediately before Hank emigrated to Australia in November 1986", Rob Bradford, *Record Collector* 124 (December 1989): *Singles 1973–1989*, 80.

1986 ?Month

#40

• LP, Reader's Digest RDS 10399:
The Shadows' Showcase

DIAMONDS[D] / CHARIOTS OF FIRE[C] / THE WINNER TAKES IT ALL[B] / MEMORY[D] / JUST THE WAY YOU ARE[A] / TEMPTATION[A] // MISTY[B] / CHI MAI[B] / IMAGINE : WOMAN[B] / THE THIRD MAN[B] / SAILING[B] / IF YOU LEAVE ME NOW[A]

Distribution
UK

****

This is an extremely rare, if not especially inspiring, item. It consists of chart-orientated covers, three from *Change Of Address* (= A), six from *Hits Right Up Your Street* (B), one from *Life In The Jungle* (C), two from *The Silver Album/ XXV* (D).

Brighton 1986
Photograph: John Hank Humphrey

Poole 31 May 1986
Photograph: David Hawley

Poole 31 May 1986
Photograph: David Hawley

1987

January 1987

#41

• CD, Polydor 815 607–2:
XXV

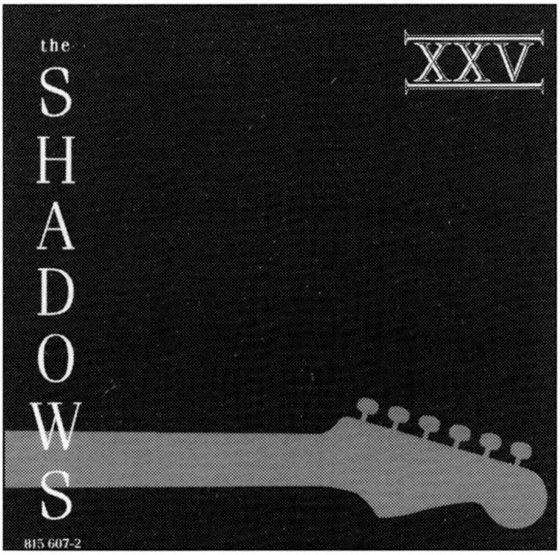

Distribution
UK, and Germany: details in *CD Guide* 114.

Running Time
46m 30s

CD issue (in "Special Price" series) of 1983 LP, see #21. This and *Hits Right Up Your Street* (next entry) were the only older Polydor Albums to be made available on CD this year: more would follow in 1989. EMI UK followed this same pattern, *String Of Hits* and *Another String Of Hot Hits And More!* appearing on CD in 1987, with a renewed assault on the back catalogue in

1989 (details in *CD Guide* 38–39). Common to all these issues is the minimalist presentation, with no annotation worth mentioning. The *XXV* CD does not even have composer credits (which appeared only on the record label of the original release: out of sight out of mind?).

Pictured here with four-page series-promotion sheet wrapped round the front inlay (see also #42). For some reason not all copies in the various outlets in the UK carried this sheet.

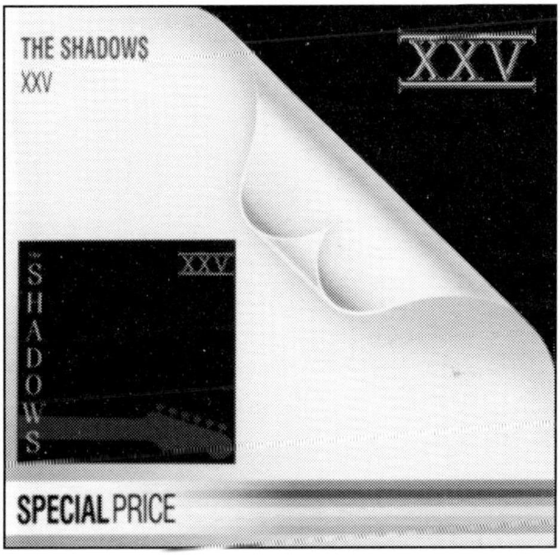

April 1987

#42

• CD, Polydor 833 452–2:
Hits Right Up Your Street

Running Time
55m 04s

UK CD issue (in "Special Price" series) of 1981 LP (#8); for a further issue, on a different label, see #68.

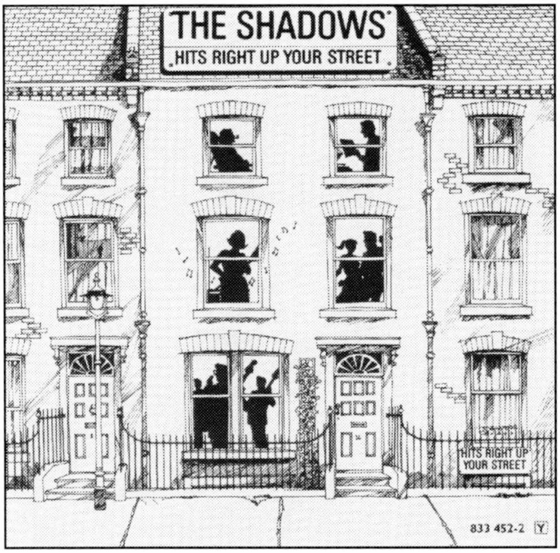

See previous entry

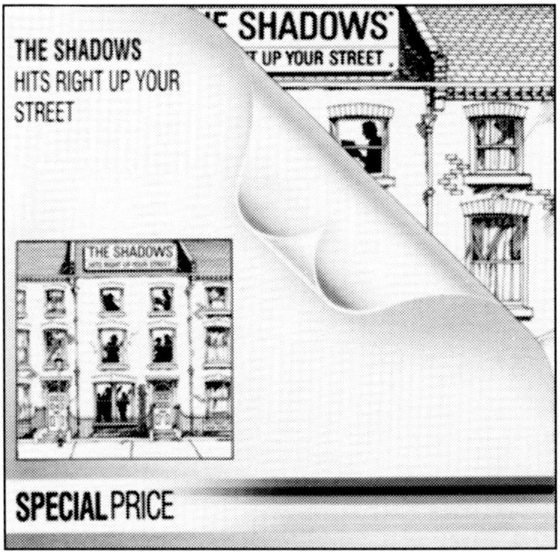

October 1987

#43

• Single, Polydor POSP 886 ~ 887 074–7:
PULASKI / CHANGE OF ADDRESS

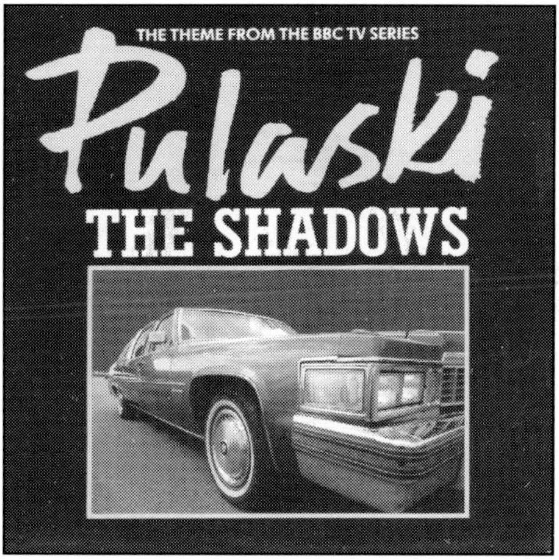

Composers
Side A: Brian Bennett
Side B: Bruce Welch, Brian Bennett, Hank Marvin

Distribution
UK only

First Appearance On CD
Side A: *Simply ... Shadows* (UK 1987) 9 (#44)
Side B: *Guitars In Love* (Holland 1987) 13 (#48)

****

See #44 for PULASKI; this was the first Polydor A-Single to feature a composition by a group-member, indeed the first since ANOTHER NIGHT for EMI in 1977. — The B-side was sourced from the 1980 Album of that name, see #2.

October 1987

#44

• LP/ CD, Polydor SHAD 1/ 833 682–1 // 833 682–2:
Simply ... Shadows

Track Listing / Composers

1 I KNEW YOU WERE WAITING (FOR ME)
Simon Climie / Dennis Morgan
2 WE DON'T NEED ANOTHER HERO
Graham Lyle / Terry Britten
3 WALKING IN THE AIR
Howard Blake
4 CARELESS WHISPER
George Michael / Andrew Ridgeley
5 DON'T GIVE UP
Peter Gabriel
6 I GUESS THAT'S WHY THEY CALL IT THE BLUES
Elton John / Bernie Taupin / Davey Johnstone
7 A HEART WILL BREAK TONIGHT
Pierre Teodori
8 THE LADY IN RED
Chris De Burgh

9 PULASKI
Brian Bennett
10 TAKE MY BREATH AWAY
Giorgio Moroder / Tom Whitlock
11 THE MUSIC OF THE NIGHT
Andrew Lloyd Webber / Charles Hart / Richard Stilgoe
12 THEMES FROM EASTENDERS & HOWARD'S WAY
Simon May / Leslie Osborne
13 I WANT TO KNOW WHAT LOVE IS
Mick Jones
14 THE SKYE BOAT SONG
Trad., arr. Cliff Hall
15 JEALOUS GUY
John Lennon
16 CHAIN REACTION
Barry, Robin & Maurice Gibb

Vocal Tracks
None

UK Chart Performance

Date of first chart entry:	24 October 1987
Highest position in chart:	*11*
Weeks in chart:	17

Top 20 Placing, *SCOFA* Poll (Polydor) 1992
No. 9 PULASKI

Distribution: LP
UK, and Germany, New Zealand, Portugal — For a South African issue see under #58

Distribution: CD
UK (also reissue 1998); for a further, budget, issue see #86

Running Time: CD
67m 34s

Associated Singles

A-side

WALKING IN THE AIR	#45
PULASKI	#43
THEMES FROM EASTENDERS & HOWARD'S WAY	#39, #46

Stage Performances

George Geddes, *On Stage* p. 11: WALKING IN THE AIR and PULASKI (1987).

****

Of the Polydor Albums to date, *Simply ... Shadows*, described as "16 brand new recordings, featuring over 60 minutes of today's classic hits", contained the highest proportion of covers of recent chart material; indeed, with the company's market research (followed up with a £300,000 television promotion campaign) now kicking in with a vengeance, all fourteen of the covers stem from the 1980s, and ten of them (in terms of peak UK/USA chart performance, twelve) from the period 1985–1987.

Without commercialism's directing hand, there might have been one or two more tracks in the mould of Brian Bennett's **PULASKI**, composed for the BBC detective series: a mellow, lyrical centrepiece framed by an energetic workout from Hank, supported by explosive synths. The other "non-hit" is outstanding too: Pierre Teodori's **A HEART WILL BREAK TONIGHT**[57] boasts a gorgeous melody; once that is dispatched, Hanks freewheels in grand style (2m 39s to the close).

The 80's chart material is, naturally enough, a mixed bag, but by no means all of it is to be written off as a best forgotten aberration in The Shadows' recording career.

The earliest original covered hit the charts big time in 1981, when Roxy Music took John Lennon's **JEALOUS GUY** to Number One. Bryan Ferry, who produced the track, preserved much of the affecting simplicity of the original, right down to the whistling, while introducing a sax. The Shadows incorporate a sax (to excess); the melody is too heavily ornamented; and the overall accompaniment, not for the only time on this Album, sounds at times leaden, at times too obtrusive for comfort.

---

[57] No connexion, aside from the title, with track 9 on Tarney-Spencer's Album *Run For Your Life* (composed by the duo).

Next in line chronologically is Elton John's 1983 No. 5 (No. 4 in the USA the year after), **I GUESS THAT'S WHY THEY CALL IT THE BLUES**. Hank's chiming guitar effectively mimics the cadences of Elton's vocal delivery, but the accompaniment scarcely does justice to the richly textured original with its vibrant backing vocals — and, of course, that harmonica solo from Stevie Wonder.

Silky smooth white soul, incisive vocals underpinned by searing sax and delicate acoustic guitar. George Michael's **CARELESS WHISPER** was a chart-topper here in 1984 (and, marketed under 'Wham! Featuring George Michael', the next year in the USA). In The Shadows' rendition of this sophisticated number, piano and guitar combine to produce one of the most satisfying tracks on *Simply ... Shadows*, with a marvellously free-flowing contribution from Hank throughout the second half.

1984 saw the release of Foreigner's gospel-tinged rock ballad **I WANT TO KNOW WHAT LOVE IS**, penned by group member (formerly of Nero and The Gladiators) Mick Jones: in 1985 it reached Number One on both sides of the Atlantic. As a specimen of lavishly produced AOR it is hard to fault. In The Shadows' hands it is a relatively restrained affair, with a sadly anaemic effort made to represent The New Jersey Mass Choir of the original! The injection of a second guitar part from Hank in the second half does little or nothing to dispel the overall impression of tedium.

Of the three further numbers that charted in 1985, one was a hit in the USA (peaking at No. 2) and in the UK (peaking at No. 3). Tina Turner's **WE DON'T NEED ANOTHER HERO**, from the soundtrack of the movie 'Mad Max Beyond Thunderdome', lends itself admirably to instrumental treatment, and The Shadows' version reflects much of the brooding intensity of the original, building to an impressively resounding climax.

A mellower high performer from 1985, **WALKING IN THE AIR**, from the 1982 30m TV cartoon 'The Snowman', took Aled Jones to No. 5 (composer Howard Blake, in a muted version featuring Peter Auty, was markedly less successful, stalling at No. 42, and in 1987 at No. 37). The combination of celestial voice and imposing orchestral accompaniment raised this piece above the level of an agreeable tune. The Shadows' shrunken production and the thinness of the sound conspire to move this track way down the list of contenders for Best Number on *Simply ... Shadows*.

Another TV-related piece, or rather one segment of two, is in a wholly different league. Simon May's **THEMES FROM EASTENDERS & HOWARDS' WAY** one way or another attained a certain amount of UK chart success in 1985/86: May's orchestra with the latter (No. 21), and, with some retitling, Marti Webb with 'Always There' (No. 13; ~ HOWARDS' WAY), Anita Dobson with 'Anyone Can Fall In Love' (No. 4; ~ EASTENDERS). The Shadows' plodding EASTENDERS is instantly forgettable, but HOWARDS' WAY, with its outstanding melody, was brilliantly interpreted by Hank on that chiming Fender. One can only marvel that nobody thought of recording this in full as a Single in its own right.[58]

The charts of 1986 generated a cluster of five cover versions. The ballad duet from Peter Gabriel and Kate Bush, **DON'T GIVE UP**, was not a notable Single hit by the standards of the *Simply ... Shadows* set, peaking at No. 9 in the UK; the parent Album however, Gabriel's *So*, was a UK No. 1 / USA No. 2. DON'T GIVE UP is a dark, brooding piece: the combination of Gabriel's forlorn cry on behalf of the masses of unemployed and Ms Bush's best efforts to inspire confidence and self-respect are affecting enough, but perhaps over-extended. The Shadows capture something of the mood of the exchange in this, the lengthiest track on the Album at five and a half minutes — but again, some trimming would have been an advantage.

Chris De Burgh's much admired romantic ballad **THE LADY IN RED** was a worldwide smash (Number One in the UK, Number Three in the USA). Hank wends his way through this one with great sensitivity, to the accompaniment of the beautifully judged drone of Alan Jones' basslines.

Los Angeles trio Berlin's **TAKE MY BREATH AWAY** was a Number One either side of the water. It was co-written for the soundtrack of the movie 'Top Gun' by Giorgio Moroder — one of his big bold "walls of sound". The Shadows rise to this one — unquestionably a fine instro in the style of the 1980s!

Presumably the immediate inspiration for **THE SKYE BOAT SONG** was the recent assault on this captivating traditional melody by Roger Whittaker[59] and Des O'Connor — a UK Number Ten. The Shadows' version is as twee

---

[58] Had this been done, The Shadows might have taken on board the forceful change of tempo, the centrepiece of the May orchestral version.

[59] Whittaker's 1986 Album *The Genius Of Love* (Tembo TMB 108) was produced by Bruce Welch; also involved were Cliff Hall, Alan Jones, Brian Bennett, Harry Bogdanovs and Tony Rivers!

as this is excruciating; there were no further group experiments with Scottish airs.

The last number covered from 1986 is Diana Ross' chart-topping (UK) **CHAIN REACTION**, a throwback to the catchy, effervescent and beat-laden songs that used to emerge from Tamla Motown when she fronted The Supremes. On this closing track (as with WALK OF LIFE, on *Moonlight Shadows*), Hank takes the opportunity to move away from the basic melody after a respectable interval and provide some slick embellishments, particularly in the final minute or so. Great fun, though not it would seem for many a deadly serious Shadows' fan.

Two numbers from 1987 remain to be considered. First, Aretha Franklin and George Michael's UK/USA chart-topper **I KNEW YOU WERE WAITING (FOR ME)**. Shads compilers habitually bypass this version, but it is hard to see why: here is Hank at his most fluent and assured as he picks his way through this 80s fusion of black and white soul. A first-rate opener.

Michael Crawford took **THE MUSIC OF THE NIGHT** only to No. 7 (though in the same year the *Phantom Of The Opera* Album hit the top). Hank uses the Morley volume pedal to good effect as he gets to grips with yet another outstanding melody from the prolific pen of Andrew Lloyd Webber.

Simply ... Shadows has not had a good press. In fact, some of the covers are creditable and a few are first-rate, as are the two "non-hits" in the collection. At the same time, the Album as a whole is (uncharacteristically for The Shadows) rather sombre, and the accompaniment at times rather heavy and forbidding, lacking sparkle; the inclusion of a couple of perkier numbers[60] would have provided a more balanced programme. The follow-up, *Steppin' To The Shadows* (#51), would offer a more satisfying mix.

---

60 My fellow-countryman George Geddes felt likewise: "The album I find a little too laid-back for my liking! I would have liked a few more up-tempo tracks", *SCOFA* 17 (1988) 19. (He also highlights TV/ radio spots, which included PULASKI and WALKING IN THE AIR.) See also Ian Kershaw, id. 21 (1989) 2.

Originals Of Cover Versions

• I KNEW YOU WERE WAITING (FOR ME)
UK Single:
Aretha Franklin & George Michael,
Epic DUET 1 (1987)
CD:
Ladies & Gentlemen:
The Best Of George Michael,
Epic 491705 2,
Disc 2/13 (1998)

• WE DON'T NEED ANOTHER HERO
UK Single:
Tina Turner,
Capitol CL 364 (1985)
CD:
Simply The Best,
Capitol CDP 79 6630 2,
track 8 (1991)

• WALKING IN THE AIR
UK Single:
Aled Jones,
HMV ALED 1 (1985)
CD:
Various Artists,
Totally Christmas,
EMI Gold 7243 8 59927 2 8,
track 14 (1997)

• CARELESS WHISPER
UK Single:
George Michael,
Epic A 4603 (1984)
CD:
Ladies ... (as above),
Disc 1/3

• DON'T GIVE UP
UK Single:
Peter Gabriel & Kate Bush,
Virgin PGS 2 (1986)
CD:
Peter Gabriel:
Sixteen Golden Greats,
Virgin Realworld 07243 8 11788 2 9,
track 7 (2002)

• I GUESS THAT'S WHY THEY CALL IT THE BLUES
UK Single:
Elton John,
Rocket XPRES 91 (1983)
CD:
Greatest Hits 1970–2002,
Mercury/ Rocket 063 449–2,
Disc 2/3 (2002)

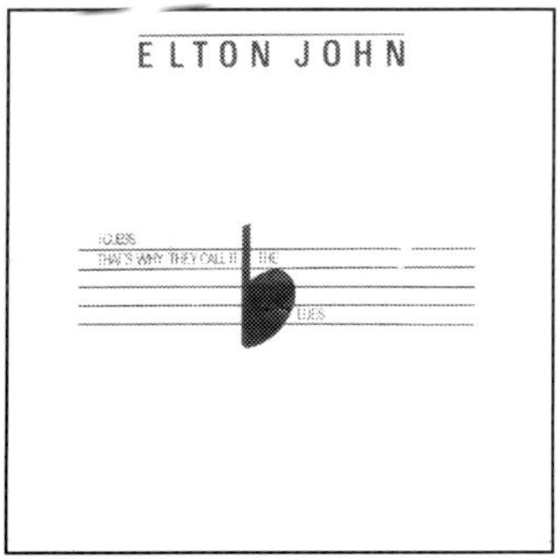

• THE LADY IN RED
UK Single:
Chris De Burgh,
A & M AM 331 (1986)
CD:
The Ultimate Collection,
Mercury 490 899–2,
track 5 (2001)

• TAKE MY BREATH AWAY
UK Single:
Berlin,
CBS A 7320 (1986)
CD:
The Best Of Berlin,
Geffen 9 24187–2,
track 4 (1988)

• THE MUSIC OF THE NIGHT
UK Single:
Michael Crawford,
Polydor POSP 803 (1987)
CD:
The Best Of Michael Crawford,
WSM 7567930812,
track 2 (2001)

• THE THEMES FROM EASTENDERS & HOWARDS' WAY

EASTENDERS:
UK Single:
Anita Dobson,
'Anyone Can Fall In Love',
BBC RESL 191 (1986)

HOWARDS' WAY:
UK Single:
Marti Webb,
'Always There',
BBC RESL 190 (1986)

HOWARDS' WAY:
UK Single:
Simon May Orchestra,
'Howards' Way',
BBC RESL 174 (1985)

• I WANT TO KNOW WHAT LOVE IS
UK Single:
Foreigner,
Atlantic A 9596 (1984)
CD:
The Definitive,
Atlantic/Rhino/WSM 8122 73596 2,
Track 3 (2002)

• THE SKYE BOAT SONG
UK Single:
Roger Whittaker & Des O'Connor,
Tembo TML 119 (1986)
CD:
Roger Whittaker,
BMG 74321 892532,
Disc 1/17 (2001)

• JEALOUS GUY
UK Singles:
Roxy Music, EG ROXY 2 (1981)
John Lennon, Parlophone R 6117 (1985)
CDs:
Bryan Ferry:
The Ultimate Collection,
EG EGCTV2, track 8 (1988)
Lennon Legend:
The Very Best Of John Lennon,
EMI 7243 8 21954 2 9, track 4 (1997)

• CHAIN REACTION
UK Single:
Diana Ross,
Capitol CL 386 (1986)
CD:
Love And Life:
The Very Best Of Diana Ross,
EMI/ Universal 7243 5 35862 2 5,
Disc 1/1 (2001)

November 1987

#45

• Single, Polydor POSP 898 ~ 887 247–7:
WALKING IN THE AIR [but see below] / OUTDIGO

Composers

Side A: Howard Blake
Side B: Bruce Welch / Brian Bennett / Hank Marvin

Distribution
UK only

First Appearance On CD
Side A: *Simply ... Shadows* (UK 1987) 3 (#44)
Side B: *Dancing In The Dark* (UK 1990/91) 11 (#62/ #64)

****

Hot on the heels of PULASKI released in October (#43) came this, the A-side from *Simply ... Shadows* (#44), marketed under the (more seasonal) title THEME FROM THE SNOWMAN. — The B-side was once again (see #43) sourced from the 1980 Album *Change Of Address* (#2).

The Shadows were now to embark upon a quiet period (taking the year 1988 off): no Polydor releases, even compilations, in the UK or anywhere else. But the market revived in 1989.

1987

#46

• Overseas Single, EMI 885:
THEMES FROM EASTENDERS & HOWARDS' WAY / GOING HOME

Issued in New Zealand, A variation on UK #39 ~ #22: the 'Eastenders' soap hit Australia in January 1987, while GOING HOME was featured on a N.Z. television commercial (*SCOFA* 14 [1987] 4 & 15 [1987] 6).

1987

#47

• Overseas LP, EMI EMC 261245:
The Shadows In The Eighties

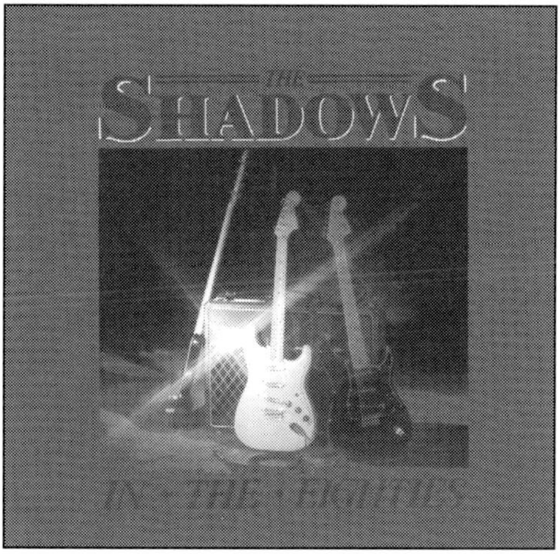

* = Polydor tracks

CLASSICAL GAS / THEME FROM THE DEER HUNTER / BRIDGE OVER TROUBLED WATER / YOU'RE THE ONE THAT I WANT / DON'T CRY FOR ME ARGENTINA / BRIGHT EYES / BAKER STREET / CHI MAI*[A] / WE DON'T TALK ANYMORE*[A] // IMAGINE : WOMAN*[A] / THIS OLE HOUSE*[A] / THEME FROM MISSING*[B] / CHARIOTS OF FIRE*[B] / AFRICA*[C] / GOING HOME*[C] / UP WHERE WE BELONG*[C] / TIME IS TIGHT*[C] / QUEEN OF HEARTS*[C]

Distribution
Australia

Vocal Tracks
None

Here is a rather confined view of the group "in the Eighties" (the Eighties taking in the 1979 *String Of Hits* which was of course a UK chart-topper in 1980). Of the eleven Polydor items on this 18-tracker, four were sourced from *Hits Right Up Your Street* (= A), two from *Life In The Jungle* (B), five from *The Silver Album/ XXV* (C). No group originals — the closest approximation to that is John Farrar's YOU'RE THE ONE THAT I WANT from *String Of Hits*.

1987

#48

• Overseas LP/ CD, Dino Music DNLP 1154 // DNCD 1154:
Guitars In Love

I JUST CALLED TO SAY I LOVE YOU[D] / HELLO[D] / IF YOU LEAVE ME NOW[A] / ALBATROSS[A] / NIGHTS IN WHITE SATIN[D] / SAILING[B] / IMAGINE : WOMAN[B] / YOU DON'T HAVE TO SAY YOU LOVE ME[C] // THE POWER OF LOVE[D] / AFRICA[C] / JUST THE WAY YOU ARE[A] / THREE TIMES A LADY[D] / CHANGE OF ADDRESS[A] / I KNOW HIM SO WELL[D] / SUMMER LOVE '59[B] / EVERY BREATH YOU TAKE[D]

CD Running Time
63m 49s

Distribution
Holland

Vocal Tracks
None

Seven of the sixteen tracks embracing the "world's most beautiful love songs" come from *Moonlight Shadows* (= D), four from *Change Of Address* (A), three from *Hits Right Up Your Street* (B), with only two from *The Silver Album/ XXV* (C). Chart material predominates; group originals are represented only by CHANGE OF ADDRESS and SUMMER LOVE '59.

This "TV-Album" entered the Dutch charts on 4 July 1987, and stayed there for 7 weeks, peaking at No. 44 (information kindly supplied by Harry de Louw).

Brighton 1987
Photograph: John Hank Humphrey

Brighton 1987
Photograph: John Hank Humphrey

1989

April 1989

#49

• Single, Polydor PO 47 ~ 889 186–7:
MOUNTAINS OF THE MOON / STACK-IT

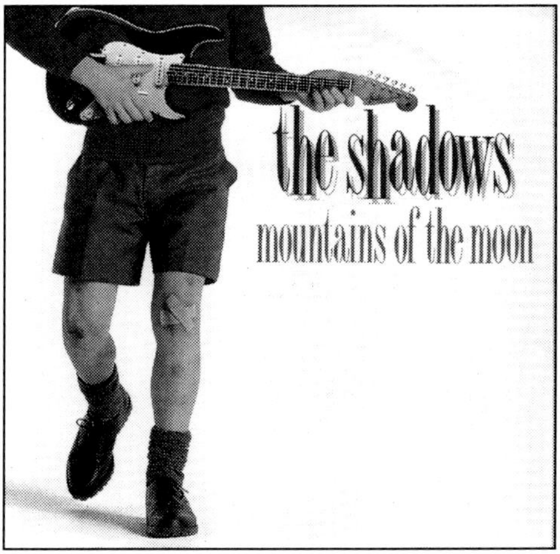

Composers
Side A: Brian Bennett
Side B: Hank Marvin / Bruce Welch / Brian Bennett

Distribution
UK only

First Appearance On CD
Sides A/B: #50 below

Both sides would appear shortly on LP/CD *Steppin' To The Shadows*, #51; see also next entry. Here was another Brian Bennett-penned A-Single (cf. PULASKI, #43), the group's penultimate.

April 1989

#50

• CD Single, Polydor PZ CD 47 ~ 889 187–2:
MOUNTAINS OF THE MOON / STACK-IT / TURNING POINT

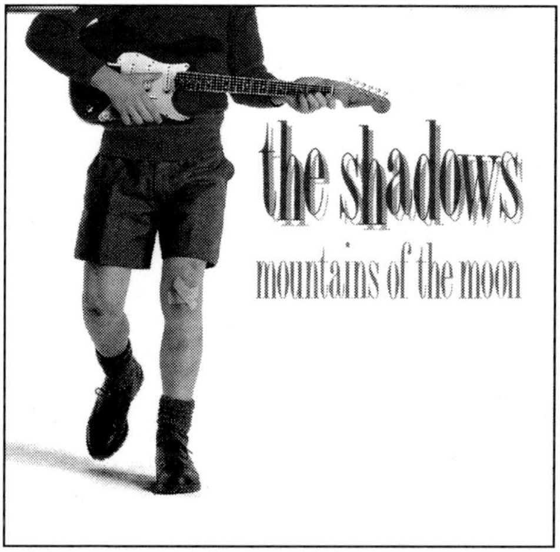

Running Time
14m 28s

UK only. The first of two Shadows' CD Singles, made available only in very limited quantities (not at all unusual among record companies at the time); for the content see previous entry (TURNING POINT from 1984 Album *Guardian Angel*, #27).

London / Sheffield 1989
Photographs: John Hank Humphrey

May 1989

#51

• LP/ CD, Polydor SHAD 30 ~ 839 357–1 // 839 357–2:
Steppin' To The Shadows

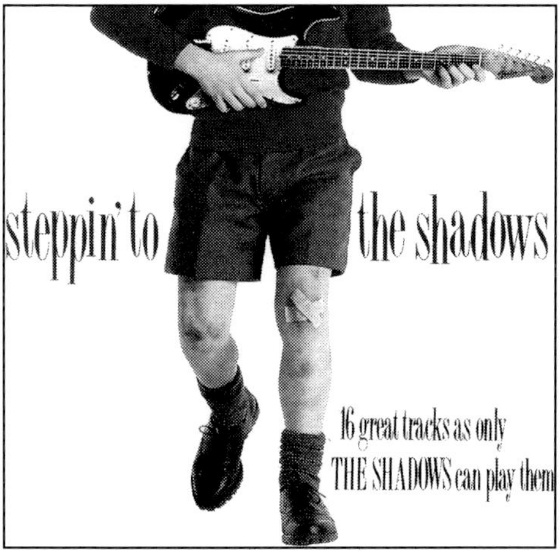

Track Listing / Composers

1 YOU WIN AGAIN
Barry, Maurice & Robin Gibb

2 I WANNA DANCE WITH SOMEBODY (WHO LOVES ME)
George Merrill / Shannon Rubicam

3 HE AIN'T HEAVY, HE'S MY BROTHER
Bob Russell / Bobby Scott

4 CANDLE IN THE WIND
Elton John / Bernie Taupin

5 FAREWELL MY LOVELY
Pierre Teodori

6 MOUNTAINS OF THE MOON
Brian Bennett

7 NOTHING'S GONNA CHANGE MY LOVE FOR YOU
Gerry Goffin / Michael Masser

8 HEAVEN IS A PLACE ON EARTH
Ellen Shipley / Rick Nowels

9 WHEN THE GOING GETS TOUGH (THE TOUGH GET GOING)
Wayne Braithwaite / Barry J Eastmond
10 ALONE
Billy Steinberg / Tom Kelly
11 ALL I ASK OF YOU
Andrew Lloyd Webber / Charles Hart
12 STACK-IT
Hank Marvin / Bruce Welch / Brian Bennett
13 SHOBA
Hank Marvin
14 YOU KEEP ME HANGIN' ON
Brian Holland / Lamont Dozier / Eddie Holland
15 SOME PEOPLE
Alan Tarney
16 ONE MOMENT IN TIME
Albert Hammond / John Bettis

Vocal Tracks

None

UK Chart Performance

Date of first chart entry:	20 May 1989
Highest position in chart:	*11*
Weeks in chart:	9

Top 20 Placing, *SCOFA* Poll (Polydor) 1992

No. 2	MOUNTAINS OF THE MOON
No. 8	STACK-IT
No. 15	FAREWELL MY LOVELY

Top 20 Placing, Best Instro 1970–1990, *Shadsfax* Poll (Polydor +) 2001

No. 6	MOUNTAINS OF THE MOON

Distribution: LP

UK, and Australasia[61], Germany, Holland, Yugoslavia

61 "Manufactured for Australasia in Australia", see John Campbell's exemplary NZ "Penumbra" Website.

Distribution: CD
UK (see further issue + reissue [budget] at #72), Australia (1989 & 1993) — Also released in Holland under a different title, see #85

Running Time: CD
69m 02s

Associated Singles
See #49, #50; also (DJ Promo) #54

Stage Performances
According to the data in George Geddes[62], *On Stage* p. 12: (1989) MOUNTAINS OF THE MOON[63], HE AIN'T HEAVY HE'S MY BROTHER, STACK-IT.

****

On *Simply ... Shadows* (#44), the concentration of chart cover versions was broken up by one group original and one number from the pen of Pierre Teodori; this time round, among a further "16 great tracks as only The Shadows can play them", the tally is three group to one Teodori.

There is no need to dwell on the splendidly executed **MOUNTAINS OF THE MOON**: Rob Bradford has provided two illuminating profiles, in the sleevenotes to the 1998 CD *Shadstrax*, and earlier in *Record Collector* No. 124 (December 1989) 80. **STACK-IT**, the creation of the three principal members of the group, is no less accomplished. Rob Bradford again (sleevenotes): "It has a really smooth, bluesy yet soulful groove to it" — over five minutes of instrumental brilliance in fact. Stylistically, Hank Marvin's **SHOBA** with its magnificent, ringing lead guitar would not have been out of place (synthesisers aside) on his eponymous 1969 solo Album. Similarly, Pierre Teodori's outstanding **FAREWELL MY LOVELY** (an inspired inclusion) is reminiscent in a general way of those vibrant, tuneful numbers which The Shadows cruised through so effortlessly in the 60s (IT'S A MAN'S WORLD and the like).

---

62 See also *SCOFA* 21 (1989) 17.
63 This one also in 1990: see the reports in *SCOFA* 25 (1990) 4, and 26 (1991) 14–15.

Passing on now to the cover versions: these, like their predecessors on *Simply ... Shadows*, are commonly given a rough ride, despite the fact that there are some cracking songs given The Shadows' treatment in this collection.

All twelve numbers enjoyed chart success (in the UK or USA or both) between the years 1986–1988, so the spread is more restricted than ever on this Album (though three of the songs were actually remakes of originals predating the 1980s). Even so, as it happens these years were especially notable for a profusion of exceptionally fine mid- to up-tempo numbers — a handful of which are represented here.

From 1986:
Billy Ocean's pop/ dance number **WHEN THE GOING GETS TOUGH**, which was featured on the soundtrack to the movie 'The Jewel Of The Nile' (UK No. 1 / USA No. 2); Kim Wilde's thoroughly contemporary-sounding remake of The Supremes' classic **YOU KEEP ME HANGIN' ON** (UK No. 2 / [1987] USA No. 1, and a big seller throughout Europe).

From 1987:
The Bee Gees' anthemic comeback Single **YOU WIN AGAIN** (UK No. 1); Whitney Houston's star-studded disco-flavoured **I WANNA DANCE WITH SOMEBODY** (UK No. 1 / USA No. 1); Belinda Carlisle's first and biggest UK Single, with its singalong chorus, **HEAVEN IS A PLACE ON EARTH** (USA No. 1 / [peaked in 1988] UK No. 1); Cliff Richard's **SOME PEOPLE** (UK No. 3).

As presented by The Shadows, SOME PEOPLE is smooth-flowing, yet it seems stripped of all emotion, lacking the warmth and spontaneity of the Cliff version. But I see little or nothing to complain about in the remainder. The superlative Billy Ocean and Bee Gees' songs come off particularly well, not least because of that gloriously full-bodied, resonant, vibrant Fender guitar (curiously not as much in evidence on the previous Album, where the lead seems too uniform soundwise and often lacking in bite). The Whitney Houston number benefits from a first-rate accompaniment, with a fine intro from Cliff Hall and a virtuoso finale from Hank Marvin, while the lively rendition of YOU KEEP ME HANGIN' ON is not by any means thrown into the shade by Kim Wilde's supercharged version.

The remaining six:

Both Cliff Richard and Sarah Brightman scored a number of conspicuous successes as duettists: their collaboration on **ALL I ASK OF YOU** from the musical 'The Phantom Of The Opera' earned them a No. 3 in 1986. The melody may not be one of Andrew Lloyd Webber's strongest, but the tonal variations in Hank's lead lines cleverly mirror the male solo/ female solo/ duetting of the original.

Heart's power ballad **ALONE** (1987 UK NO. 3 / USA No. 1) is a hard act to follow, since much of its impact stems from Ann Wilson's compelling lead vocal. The Shadows' account seems wooden by comparison — as if threatening to run out of steam any moment after the first couple of minutes.

Much more free-flowing and expressive is the rendition of The Hollies' **HE AIN'T HEAVY, HE'S MY BROTHER** (reissued after exposure on a TV beer advert, a UK Number One — amazingly only their second — in 1988). The accompaniment loses out a little to the original's cascading strings and subdued but effective piano (from session-man Elton John).

Very different in execution is The Shadows' interpretation of **CANDLE IN THE WIND**, a live version of which (with support from The Melbourne Symphony Orchestra) took Elton John to UK No. 5 and USA No. 6 in 1988. This striking instrumental version comes over as very flamboyant — almost swaggering at times.[64] Technically impressive, if not true to the spirit of the original, from a less demonstrative than usual Elton.

Glenn Medeiros seems a minor light in comparison with the celebritites visited on this Album; he did however secure a Number One in the UK in 1988 (Number Twelve in the USA) with the romantic ballad **NOTHING'S GONNA CHANGE MY LOVE FOR YOU** (aired by George Benson in 1985); not exactly mesmerising stuff, either in the original or in the cover; in fact, the lead guitar ir rather too forward and even strident in the closing stages — no cure for an incurably dull song.

Lastly, another serving of Whitney, this time a ballad, **ONE MOMENT IN TIME** (UK No. 1 / USA No. 5), the stirring and melodious title-track to the 1988 Olympics musical tribute. The Shadows — Hank in particular — really

---

64 Put another way: "... the melody line gets a little complicated ..." (Ian Kershaw, *SCOFA* 21 [1989] 2)!

rise to the occasion as well, producing a scaled-down but nonetheless imposing soundstage, particularly as the track draws to a close.

The incorporation of four "non-hits" gives this Album something of a head-start over *Simply ... Shadows* (#44): there are some mediocre covers on *Steppin'* too, though less of them; there are some first-class covers too; and there is greater stylistic and tonal[65] variety.

Originals Of Cover Versions

• YOU WIN AGAIN
UK Single:
The Bee Gees,
Warner Bros W 8351 (1987)
CD:
Their Greatest Hits — The Record,
Polydor 589 449–2,
Disc 2/12 (2001)

• I WANNA DANCE WITH SOMEBODY (WHO LOVES ME)
UK Single:
Whitney Houston,
Arista RIS 1 (1987)
CD:
Whitney,
Arista 258 141,
track 1 (1987)

65 The disappointing lack of variety in the sound of the lead guitar on the earlier Album was highlighted by Phil Davey in *SCOFA* 17 (1988) 5.

• HE AIN'T HEAVY, HE'S MY BROTHER
UK Single:
The Hollies,
EMI EM 74 (reissue 1988)
CD:
The Air That I Breathe:
The Very Best Of The Hollies,
EMI 0777 7 89069 2 6,
track 6 (1993)

• CANDLE IN THE WIND
UK Single:
Elton John,
Rocket EJS 15 (1988)
CD:
Elton John Live In Australia,
Mercury 558 447 2,
track 11 (1988)

• NOTHING'S GONNA CHANGE MY LOVE FOR YOU
UK Single:
Glenn Medeiros,
London LON 184 (1988)

• HEAVEN IS A PLACE ON EARTH
UK Single:
Belinda Carlisle,
Virgin VS 1036 (1987)
CD:
A Place On Earth: The Greatest Hits,
Virgin 7243 8 48470 2 9,
Disc 1/1 (1999)

• WHEN THE GOING GETS TOUGH (THE TOUGH GET GOING)
UK Single:
Billy Ocean,
Jive JIVE 114 (1986)
CD:
Life (Love Is Forever),
Jive RecordsBO CD 2–01516532,
track 2 (1997)

• ALONE
UK Single:
Heart,
Capitol CL 448 (1987)
CD:
Greatest Hits,
Capitol 7243 5 27128 2 3,
track 6 (2000)

• ALL I ASK OF YOU
UK Single:
Cliff Richard
& Sarah Brightman, Polydor POSP 802 (1986)
CD:
Cliff Richard: Private Collection,
EMI CDP 7913702,
track 3 (1988)

• YOU KEEP ME HANGIN' ON
UK Single:
Kim Wilde,
MCA KIM 4 (1986)
CD:
The Very Best Of Kim Wilde,
EMI 7243 5 35957 2 2,
track 9 (2001)

• SOME PEOPLE
UK Single:
Cliff Richard,
EMI EM 18 (1987)
CD:
The Whole Story — His Greatest Hits,
EMI 7243 5 29322 2 1,
Disc 2/8 (2000)

• ONE MOMENT IN TIME
UK Single:
Whitney Houston,
Arista 111613 (1988)
CD:
The Greatest Hits,
Arista 74321–75739–2,
Disc 1/3 (2000)

May 1989

#52

• CD, Polydor 839 348–2:
Life In The Jungle

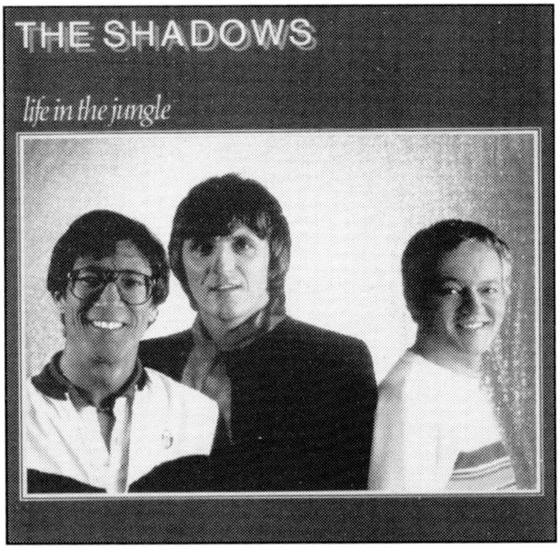

Running Time
44m 59s

CD Issue of 1982 LP, see #14, and also next entry.

May 1989

#53

• CD, Polydor 839 349–2:
Live At Abbey Road

Running Time
43m 06s

CD issue of 1982 LP, see #15; however, "all spoken references to a free album are edited out" (Jim Nugent, *Pipeline* 19 [1993] 10). The release of this Album and of *Life In The Jungle* (#52) on CD left only *Change Of Address* (#?) undigitised[66]: that would have to wait till 1992.

July 1989

#54

Promo Single, Polydor PO 52 DJ:
HE AIN'T HEAVY HE'S MY BROTHER / STACK-IT*

* Listed as SHOBA

66 Leaving aside *The Silver Album* (#19), a one-off mail-order product.

Both tracks from *Steppin' ...*, see #51. Presumably this Promo was put forward as a possible release in the wake of The Hollies' No. 1 with the reissue of HE AIN'T HEAVY ... in 1988. In the event, something quite different would be issued five months further on (next entry).

December 1989 ~ Reissue September 1990

#55

• Single Polydor PO 61 ~ 873 344–7
•• CD Single PZCD 61 ~ 873 345–2:
SHADOWMIX / ARTY'S PARTY

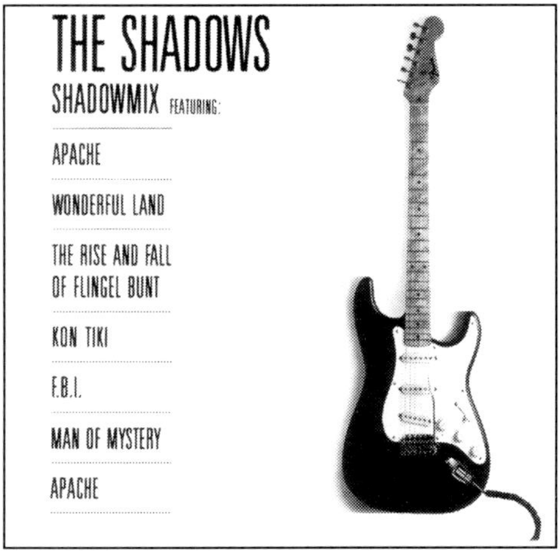

Composers
A: Various, see under #56.
B: Bruce Welch / Brian Bennett / Hank Marvin

Distribution
UK

First Appearance On CD // CD Running Time
A/B: this issue // 8m 23s

See on #59 (A-side) and #2 (B-side). The last Shadows' Single released commercially. SHADOWMIX was not nearly as impressive as the 12" DANCING IN THE DARK remix described in #38 above: a contrived, overpowering drumbeat for the track's duration, together with a short verbal intro ("Ladies and gentlemen ..."!) takes us into snatches of the revamped hits, APACHE, WONDERFUL LAND, THE RISE AND FALL OF FLINGEL BUNT, KON-TIKI, FBI, MAN OF MYSTERY, then back to APACHE with overdubbed applause. Certainly not a Golden Great; in fact, Alan Taylor's verdict (*Pipeline* 5 [1990] 32), "It's all rather a mess really", does not seem unduly harsh.

December 1989 **#56** • LP/ CD, Polydor 841 520–1 // 841 520–2: *The Shadows At Their Very Best*

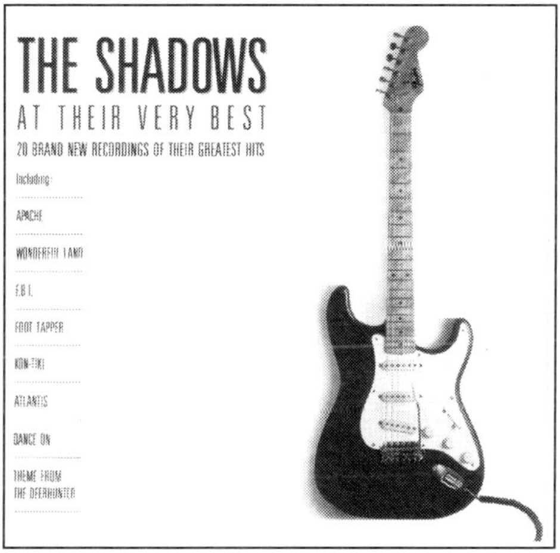

Track Listing / Composers

1 APACHE
Jerry Lordan

2 MAN OF MYSTERY
Michael Carr

3 SHINDIG
Hank Marvin / Bruce Welch
4 WONDERFUL LAND
Jerry Lordan
5 THE RISE AND FALL OF FLINGEL BUNT
Bruce Welch / Hank Marvin / John Rostill / Brian Bennett
6 THEME FROM THE DEER HUNTER
Stanley Myers
7 THE BOYS
Brian Bennett / Bruce Welch / Hank Marvin
8 THE FRIGHTENED CITY
Norrie Paramor
9 THEME FOR YOUNG LOVERS
Bruce Welch
10 DANCE ON!
Val & Elaine Murtagh / Ray Adams
11 THE SAVAGE
Norrie Paramor
12 FBI
Peter Gormley[67]
13 GUITAR TANGO
Norman Maine / Georges Liferman
14 GENIE WITH THE LIGHT BROWN LAMP
Hank Marvin / Bruce Welch / Brian Bennett / John Rostill
15 ATLANTIS
Jerry Lordan
16 FOOT TAPPER
Hank Marvin / Bruce Welch
17 DON'T CRY FOR ME ARGENTINA
Tim Rice / Andrew Lloyd Webber
18 KON-TIKI
Michael Carr
19 GERONIMO
Hank Marvin
20 THE STRANGER
Bill Crompton / Morgan 'Thunderclap' Jones

Vocal Tracks
None

[67] But see *The Shadows At EMI* p. 83.

UK Chart Performance

Date of first chart entry:	16 December 1989
Highest position in chart:	*12*
Weeks in chart:	9

Distribution: LP

UK, and Australasia[68], Holland, South Africa

Distribution: CD

UK (also reissue 1994), Mexico

Running Time: CD

52m 43s

Stage Performances

On the basis of the data assembled by George Geddes, *On Stage* pp. 9–12, most of these classic numbers were performed during the 1980s as follows[69] (no entry for 1988, which was an "empty" year):

• 1980 through to 1989: APACHE*, WONDERFUL LAND*, THE RISE AND FALL OF FLINGEL BUNT*, THEME FROM THE DEER HUNTER*, THE FRIGHTENED CITY*, FBI*, FOOT TAPPER*, DON'T CRY FOR ME ARGENTINA*

• Throughout with minor exceptions:

Not 1986:	ATLANTIS*
Not 1982/83:	KON-TIKI*
Not 1982/83/86:	DANCE ON!*

• Others:

SHINDIG (1982/83), THE STRANGER* (1987/89), MAN OF MYSTERY (1980), THE BOYS (1985: Australia!), THEME FOR YOUNG LOVERS (1983), GUITAR TANGO* (1980)

• No representation:

THE SAVAGE, GENIE WITH THE LIGHT BROWN LAMP, GERONIMO

Those asterisked above were performed also in 1990 (see reports in *SCOFA* 25 [1990] 4 and 26 [1991] 14–15).

68 "Manufactured for Australasia in Australia", see John Campbell, NZ "Penumbra" Website.

69 Listed in the order of the tracks on *At Their Very Best*.

The making of this Album gave The Shadows at a stroke the means to issue compilations on Polydor incorporating the numbers with which they will forever be most strongly associated.[70] So, in September 1992, Polydor/Polytel could market a substantial collection under the title *Complete* which had APACHE as well as THE LADY IN RED, THE STRANGER as well as DANCING IN THE DARK. In October 1994 *The Best Of Hank Marvin And The Shadows* kicked off with EVERY BREATH YOU TAKE, and went on with THE RISE AND FALL OF FLINGEL BUNT — and so on.

Given the targeted market, it came as no surprise to find that the originals were followed reasonably faithfully[71], more so in general than they were in the group's 80s concert appearances.[72] What is missing in these new versions of course is the wide variation in "that sound" as it evolved over the successive releases of the 1960s and beyond. In fact, sophistication and polish largely take over from raw energy and bite: contrast for instance the two versions of THE FRIGHTENED CITY or THE SAVAGE.

There is another dissimilarity: for the most part the remakes possess a relatively narrow Stereo spread[73], so these are not "in your face" versions, quite the reverse; in particular, that distinctive rhythm guitar is now not nearly as conspicuous. In addition, Mark Griffiths' basslines seem to lack spontaneity — not good news when faced with originals as individual in this department as KON-TIKI and THE RISE AND FALL ... Finally, was it really necessary to have WONDERFUL LAND (*such* a classic, after all) *without* strings attached? It is not as if 80's groups were entirely dominated by keyboards, and surely the help of a string section (and a bit more) could have been enlisted without undue difficulty. As it is, the characteristic brilliance and thrust of Norrie Paramor's accompaniment is sorely missed here.

---

[70] This point was emphasised by Mike Lloyd in *Pipeline* 5 (1990) 7, though he is surely wide of the mark in talking of "almost imperceptible differences".
[71] There are of course variations, usually but not invariably minor — notably in THE RISE AND FALL OF FLINGEL BUNT, FBI, GUITAR TANGO, and (more adventurously) GENIE WITH THE LIGHT BROWN LAMP; and, above all, the finale of THE STRANGER, closing up the Album with something of a flourish.
[72] This is not to say that 80's practice is not relevant to these recordings: it is a question of degree. — See on this point, and on the philosophy behind these new cuts, the remarks of Bruce Welch, liner notes to 2001 CD *The Hit Sound Of The Shadows* (#92 below).
[73] One very notable exception is THEME FOR YOUNG LOVERS, where however the enveloping keyboard accompaniment serves to drain away much of the original's vigour and vitality (not that the original was ideally put together, as is well known).

One surprising omission was RIDERS IN THE SKY[74], but a new version of that would surface in 1990 (#59).

December 1989

#57

• LP/ CD,

Pickwick CN 2104 // PWKS 559 [also in 1990 CD BOX see #62]:

The Shadows Collection

JUST THE WAY YOU ARE[A] / TURNING POINT[C] / MIDNIGHT CREEPIN'[A] / THE SHADY LADY[E] / THING-ME-JIG[B] / JOHNNY STACCATO[C] / STACK-IT[D] / IF YOU LEAVE ME NOW[A] // EQUINOXE (PART V)[A] / CHANGE OF ADDRESS[A] / FENDER BENDER[E] / TEMPTATION[A] / THE FOURTH MAN[E] / SUMMER LOVE '59[B] / MOZART FORTE[A] / ALBATROSS[A]

Vocal Tracks

None

[74] More important in the grand scheme of things, one would have thought, than GERONIMO.

Distribution
UK

CD Running Time
60m 53s

This sixteen-track compilation, which included a high proportion of group compositions, was of special interest to collectors of The Shadows on CD: five of the tracks were already available on this format via *Hits Right Up Your Street* (= B), *Guardian Angel* [75](C) (for the relatively few who actually purchased a copy!), and *Steppin' To The Shadows* (D); however, a further eight were sourced from *Change Of Address* (A), which would not be transferred to CD until 1992; in addition, there were three B-sides (E) which were not available anywhere else: FENDER BENDER from 1980 (#4), THE FOURTH MAN from 1981 (#6), THE SHADY LADY from 1982 (#13). — Also on offer was a sketch (uncredited) of the group's career to date.

Regrettably, the chemical composition of this CD, together with further CDs in the series, was to prove problematic: see *CD Guide* 269 (postscript to note 49).

See further on #62 [CD Box Set].

1989

#58

• Overseas 2 LP, Polydor MMTL 1459/60:
Moonlight Shadows / Simply ... Shadows

Issued in South Africa. See under #36 and #44; "The pictures of this gatefold sleeve are the same as those released elsewhere, but inside one panel has a picture of burnt countryside and clouds", Ian Kershaw in *SCOFA* 23 (1990).

75 One of the two numbers from this Album, JOHNNY STACCATO, was reduced for this Pickwick release from 3m 50s to 2m 31s: see *CD Guide* 177. It is hard to see why this was allowed to happen. The CD's running time is just under 61m, well below the allowable limit; the LP equivalent is pretty long by vinyl standards, but hardly unmanageable.

Sheffield 1989
Photograph: John Hank Humphrey

Sheffield 1989
Photograph: John Hank Humphrey

1990

September 1990

#59

• LP/ CD, Polydor 847 120–1 // 847 120–2:
Reflection

Track Listing / Composers

1 EYE OF THE TIGER
Frank Sullivan / Jim Peterik

2 CROCKETT'S THEME
Jan Hammer

3 RIGHT HERE WAITING
Richard Marx

4 EVERY LITTLE THING SHE DOES IS MAGIC
Sting

5 SEALED WITH A KISS
Gary Geld / Peter Udell
6 UPTOWN GIRL
Billy Joel
7 STRAWBERRY FIELDS FOREVER
John Lennon / Paul McCartney
8 RIDERS IN THE SKY '90
Stan Jones //
9 FLASHDANCE ... WHAT A FEELING
Giorgio Moroder / Keith Forsey / Irene Cara
10 SOMETHING'S GOTTEN HOLD OF MY HEART
Roger Greenaway / Roger Cook
11 LOVE CHANGES EVERYTHING
Andrew Lloyd Webber / Don Black / Charles Hart
12 NOTHING'S GONNA STOP US NOW
Diane Warren / Albert Hammond
13 BILITIS
Francis Lai
14 YOU'LL NEVER WALK ALONE
Richard Rodgers / Oscar Hammerstein II
15 SHADOWMIX
Various, see #56
16 ALWAYS ON MY MIND
Wayne Thompson / Mark James / John Christopher

Vocal Tracks
None

UK Chart Performance

Date of first chart entry:	13 October 1990
Highest position in chart:	5
Weeks in chart:	15

Top 20 Placing, *SCOFA* Poll (Polydor) 1992

No. 4	CROCKETT'S THEME
No. 19	RIDERS IN THE SKY '90

Distribution: LP
UK, and Australasia[76], Portugal, South Africa, Zimbabwe

Distribution: CD
UK, and Australia

Running Time: CD
58m 47s

Associated Single / CD Single
(A-side) SHADOWMIX, see #55 (where note September 1990 reissue to promote Album)

****

Reflection has been much more favourably judged than either *Simply ... Shadows* (#44) or *Steppin' To The Shadows* (#51) — ironic, given that the only group compositions this time were embedded in the frivolous **SHADOWMIX** (see on #55). With the exception of the smooth-flowing (and highly imitative, though none the worse for that) rendition of Francis Lai's **BILITIS**, the title-track of the 1977 movie, it is recast chart material all the way (though six of the fourteen were themselves remakes of hits from the 1960s and 1970s).

Nonetheless, *Reflection* is indisputably of a consistently higher quality than these maligned predecessors. Quite apart from the choice of material, tonal variations in the lead instrument are exploited much more extensively, both from one number to another, and within individual numbers (SEALED WITH A KISS and CROCKETT'S THEME are notable examples of the latter).

Taking the 80's chart material in chronological order, the earliest marks a long overdue return to the group's own UK No. 12 hit of 1980. This Polydor remake is surely the best **RIDERS IN THE SKY**[77] of the three studio recordings: the EMI Album version (on *String Of Hits*) has a curiously dissonant intro and sounds forced at times; the rejigged EMI Single is livelier, but is not done any favours by the interpolation of some pretty bland "disco" effects.[78]

---

76 "Manufactured for Australasia in Australia": see John Campbell, NZ "Penumbra" Website.
77 It was arranged by Alan Jones: *SCOFA* 34 (1995) 3–4, 35 (1996) 12.
78 See on both these versions *The Shadows At EMI* 362/ 367–8. The Ramrods of course had an instro hit with this in 1961 (incorporating a snatch of APACHE filched from Jorgen Ingmann's USA smash). Not at all to my taste, but it is highly

The group had a profitable brush with The Police on *Moonlight Shadows* (#36) with EVERY BREATH YOU TAKE from 1983. This time round they took on, with equal success, an earlier piece (1981), one of the tracks drawn from the chart-topping LP *Ghost In The Machine*, the jaunty **EVERY LITTLE THING SHE DOES IS MAGIC**[79] (UK No. 1/ USA No. 3). This is a brightly-lit production, with some nifty soloing from Hank towards the close as a variation on the original's boisterous finale.

EYE OF THE TIGER, written as a theme for Sylvester Stallone's 'Rocky III' movie, with its pounding drumbeat and charged vocal delivery, took hard-rock group Survivor to the top both in the USA and the UK in 1982. The Shadows give as good as they get and better with a powerhouse version which must surely count as one of their very finest 80s covers. A magnificent opener.

The high-performing hits chosen from 1983 also furnished worthwhile instrumentals. The Shadows' version of Billy Joel's **UPTOWN GIRL** (UK No. 1/ USA No. 3) has something of the effervescence of the 60s about it — in fact the number was written by Joel as a tribute to The Four Seasons.

Giorgio Moroder composed the music (as opposed to the lyrics) for **FLASHDANCE ... WHAT A FEELING**, for the 1983 movie 'Flashdance', which vocalist Irene Cara took to Number Two in the UK and Number One in the USA. In true Moroder fashion, a subdued intro gives way to an explosive main theme — as with EYE OF THE TIGER, so with this The Shadows are true to the dynamism of the original — after the 3m mark we are almost back in the era of The Hank Marvin Guitar Syndicate at their most high-powered.

Presumably **YOU'LL NEVER WALK ALONE** was picked up by the marketing people at Polydor because it had been a UK chart-topper in 1985 for the charity venture by The Crowd, with Gerry Marsden as lead vocalist. This Rodgers and Hammerstein song from the show 'Carousel' had of course enjoyed (and would go on to enjoy) star treatment, with memorable versions from Gerry and The Pacemakers and from Elvis Presley, not to mention supporters of Liverpool FC. The Shadows though play it distinctly cool —

---

rated by many: see for an enthusiastic appreciation Tony Gowing in *Pipeline* 47 (2000) 24.

[79] Performed on stage in the course of 1990 (together with CROCKETT'S THEME and, of course, RIDERS IN THE SKY): see the reports in *SCOFA* 25 (1990) 4 and 26 (1991) 14–15.

too cool in fact — and do not go in for the uplifting approach. One of the less appealing numbers in this set.

1987 brought material for three tracks on *Reflection*: **CROCKETT'S THEME**, one of Czech keyboard player Jan Hammer's contributions to the TV series 'Miami Vice', was a UK Number Two. The Shadows really attack this one with relish: in their hands it is appropriately mean-sounding and has terrific clout, making Hammer sound almost insipid in comparison, particularly in the first half.

Hank Marvin surpasses himself on **NOTHING'S GONNA STOP US NOW**, such is his inventiveness and dexterity. He is off to a flying start admittedly with material of this calibre, a superb power ballad from Starship (UK No. 1/ USA No. 1), featured in the movie 'Mannequin'.

The impression created by the cover of **ALWAYS ON MY MIND** is quite different. Here is a version clearly founded on that of The Pet Shop Boys (UK No. 1 [1987] / USA No. 4 [1988]) rather than on the Elvis rendition: great tune, great guitar sound, shame about the hurdy-gurdy accompaniment[80] — so unadventurous and uninspired when set against that awesome hit Single, which possesses an almost symphonic dimension.

From 1989, four numbers come into the picture. Chicago-born Richard Marx has enjoyed more success in his home country than in this, but his piano-led ballad **RIGHT HERE WAITING** fared exceptionally well, reaching No. 1 in the USA and No. 2 in the UK. A superb melody, beautifully handled by Hank. —Ditto for another UK No. 2, Michael Ball's **LOVE CHANGES EVERYTHING**, from the Andrew Lloyd Webber musical 'Aspects Of Love'.

Finally here, two UK chart-toppers, both of them remakes: the much-covered **SEALED WITH A KISS** referred to earlier in this survey, from Pete Waterman protégé Jason Donovan; and **SOMETHING'S GOTTEN HOLD OF MY HEART**, from Marc Almond and Gene Pitney: shorn of the outrageous histrionics, this latter works well as an instrumental, with the ringing Marvin guitar given plenty of room to breathe.

80 " ... a really tacky latin rhythm of the sort you would find on a child's keyboard" is Alan Taylor's verdict, *Pipeline* 8 (1991) 16.

Enough of the UK population were taken with Candy Flip's funky electronic update of **STRAWBERRY FIELDS FOREVER** to lift it to Number Three by the last day of March 1990. Presumably it was this renewed interest that prompted its inclusion on *Reflection*. Or maybe not. Certainly there is nothing in The Shadows' version that approximates to Candy Flip's meanderings. Theirs is a big, bold, sweeping production, which recreates some of the rich textures of the original masterpiece; but the overall effect is too upbeat (in contrast to the ever so sombre outro) — the addition of a cellist or two would have served to darken the tone.[81]

With *Reflection* then, their very last Album of fresh material, the group came up trumps.

The recording sessions for Polydor product were so focused that there was nothing to spare — there would be no more treasures belatedly seeing the light of day. Since 1990, apart from a rogue DANCING IN THE DARK (see #91), only a live Album (#93) has been added to the tally, and even that was already accessible to the public via alternative channels.

Originals Of Cover Versions

• EYE OF THE TIGER
UK Single:
Survivor,
Scotti Brothers SCT A 2411 (1982)
CD:
Eye Of The Tiger,
Scotti Brothers 512 025–2,
track 1 (1990)

[81] Precisely this point could be made about the prior "Take 7 and edit piece" presented on The Beatles' *Anthology 2*, Disc 2/3. — All this said, The Shadows' version goes far beyond the merely ornamental workout by The Ventures on their 1967 Album *Super Psychedelics*.

• CROCKETT'S THEME
UK Single:
Jan Hammer,
MCA MCA 1193 (1987)
CD:
Escape From Television,
MCA MCLD 19133,
track 1 (1991)

• RIGHT HERE WAITING
UK Single:
Richard Marx,
EMI–USA MT 72 (1989)
CD:
Greatest Hits,
Capitol 7243 821914 2 1,
track 16 (1997)

• EVERY LITTLE THING SHE DOES IS MAGIC
UK Single:
The Police,
A & M AMS 8174 (1981)
CD:
The Very Best
Of Sting And The Police,
A & M 493 252–2,
track 9 (2002)

• SEALED WITH A KISS
UK Single:
Jason Donovan,
PWL PWL 39 (1989)
CD:
The Very Best Of Jason Donovan,
Music Club MCCD 397,
track 5 (1999)

• UPTOWN GIRL
UK Single:
Billy Joel,
CBS A 3775 (1983)
CD:
The Ultimate Collection,
Columbia Sony TV98 CD,
Disc 2/1 (2000)

• STRAWBERRY FIELDS FOREVER
UK Single:
(PENNY LANE / STRAWBERRY ...)
The Beatles, Parlophone R 5570 (1967)
Candy Flip, Debut DEBT 3092 (1990)
CD:
The Beatles 1967–1970,
EMI/ Apple 0777 7 97039 2 0,
Disc 1/1 (1993)

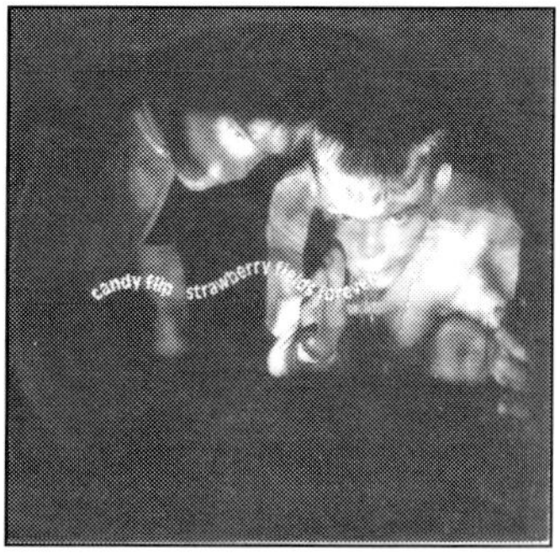

• RIDERS IN THE SKY '90
UK Single:
The Shadows,
EMI 5027 (1980)
CD:
The Original Chart Hits 1960–1980,
EMI CDS 7937522,
Disc 2/20 (1990)

• FLASHDANCE ... WHAT A FEELING
UK Single:
Irene Cara,
Casablanca CAN 1016 (1983)
CD:
Soundtrack 'Flashdance',
Casablanca 811 492–2,
track 1 (n.d.)

• SOMETHING'S GOTTEN HOLD OF MY HEART
UK Single:
Marc Almond & Gene Pitney,
Parlophone R 6201 (1989)
CD:
Gene Pitney: The Ultimate Collection,
Castle Music NEECD 380,
Disc 2/25 (2001)

• LOVE CHANGES EVERYTHING
UK Single:
Michael Ball,
Really Useful RUR 3 (1989)
CD:
The Best Of Michael Ball,
Polydor 523 891–2,
track 4 (1994)

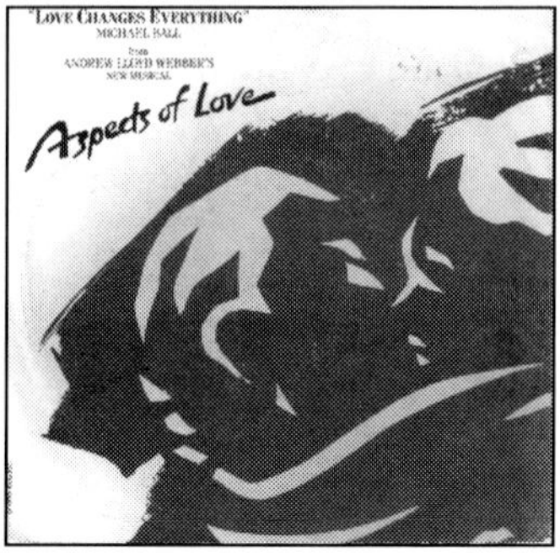

• NOTHING'S GONNA STOP US NOW
UK Single:
Starship,
Grunt FB 49757 (1987)
CD:
Greatest Hits
(Ten Years And Change 1979–1991),
BMG 74321 28990 2 2,
track 9 (1991)

• BILITIS
CD:
The Love Collection:
Francis Lai and Michel Legrand,
Bianco Music & Entertainment
BIA21010,
Disc 1/1 (2000)

• YOU'LL NEVER WALK ALONE
UK Single:
The Crowd,
Spartan BRAD 1 (1985)
CD:
(Gerry And The Pacemakers)
Best Of The 60s,
Disky S1 250732,
track 6 (2000)

• ALWAYS ON MY MIND
UK Single:
The Pet Shop Boys,
Parlophone R 6171 (1987)
CD:
Discography,
EMI 7979942,
track 8 (1991)

September 1990

#60

• LP/ CD, Pickwick PWK LPS 4018 P // PWKS 4018 P:
Diamonds

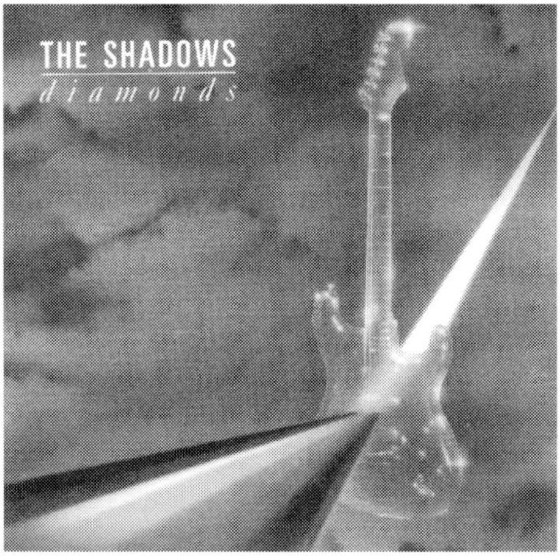

DIAMONDS[D] / IMAGINE : WOMAN[B] / THEME FROM MISSING[C] / YOU RESCUE ME[C] / HATS OFF TO WALLY[B] / NUT ROCKER[B] / GUARDIAN ANGEL[E] / UP WHERE WE BELONG[D] // THIS OLE HOUSE[B] / AFRICA[D] / ARTY'S PARTY[A] / CAN'T PLAY YOUR GAME[E] / THE OLD ROMANTICS[C] / OUR ALBERT[E] / COWBOY CAFE[B] / WE DON'T TALK ANYMORE[B]

Vocal Tracks
4, 7, 12

Distribution
UK

CD Running Time
61m 49s

A second eclectic sixteen-tracker from Pickwick, with an enthusiastic appreciation of the group from John Tobler (see #57 for the previous collection): one track from *Change Of Address* (= A), six from *Hits Right Up Your Street* (B), three from *Life In The Jungle* (C), three from *The Silver Album/ XXV* (D), three from *Guardian Angel* (E). Only one of these Albums, the first, was so far unobtainable on CD (with two of its numbers, INDIGO and OUTDIGO, still undigitised).

Six group compositions were included. A good selection overall.

See further on #62 (CD Box Set).

November 1990

#61

• LP/ CD, Reader's Digest RDS 10709 // RDCD 157:
Relaxing With The Shadows

* Denotes Polydor tracks:

THE THIRD MAN* / SAILING* / SUPERSTAR / SOMETHING / JUST THE WAY YOU ARE* / CATHY'S CLOWN / A WHITER SHADE OF PALE* / CHARIOTS OF FIRE* // GOODBYE YELLOW BRICK ROAD / YOU DON'T HAVE TO SAY YOU LOVE ME* / TRAINS AND BOATS AND PLANES / UP WHERE WE BELONG* / BRIDGE OVER TROUBLED WATER / LET IT BE ME

Vocal Tracks
Last track only [EMI]

Distribution
UK

CD Running Time
51m 52s

****

This "special programme" was a bonus for purchasers of The RD Box Set *Great Romantic Hits Of The 70s & 80s*. Of the seven Polydor tracks, JUST THE WAY YOU ARE was sourced from *Change Of Address*, THE THIRD MAN and SAILING from *Hits Right Up Your Street*, CHARIOTS OF FIRE from *Life In The Jungle*, and A WHITER SHADE OF PALE, YOU DON'T HAVE TO SAY YOU LOVE ME and UP WHERE WE BELONG from *The Silver Album/ XXV*.

No room was found, naturally enough, for group compositions.

Nottingham 1990
Photograph: John Hank Humphrey

December 1990

#62

• 3 CD Set , Pickwick BOXD 8 ~ 101 008 2:
A Special Collection

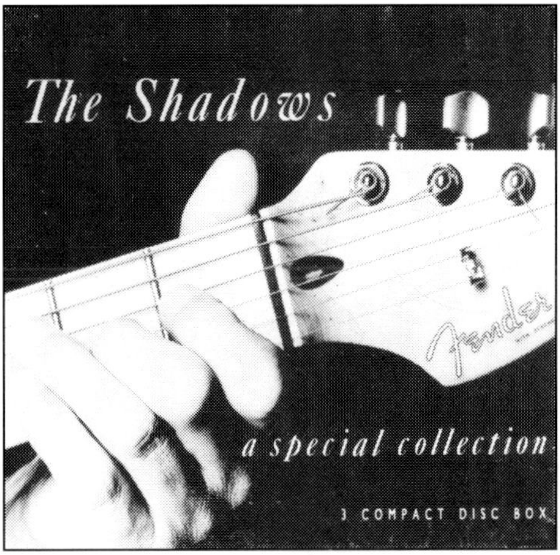

This UK 3CD set comprises *The Shadows Collection, Diamonds* and *Dancing In The Dark;* all were released singly also, the first in December 1989, the second in September 1990, the third prospectively, in February 1991. See under #57, 60 and 64 for individual descriptions.

The 48 tracks in question were sourced as follows:

Change Of Address
8 + 1 + 1 = 10
Hits Right Up Your Street
2 + 6 + 2 = 10
Life In The Jungle
0 + 3 + 4 = 7
Silver Album/ XXV
0 + 3 + 3 = 6
Guardian Angel
2 + 3 + 1 = 6
Moonlight Shadows
0 + 0 + 1 = 1
Steppin' To The Shadows
1 + 0 + 2 = 3
B-sides
3 + 0 + 2 = 5

As remarked in *CD Guide* 265, there is a nearly complete run of B-Singles from FENDER BENDER in 1980 to ARTY'S PARTY in 1989; nearly complete, because JOHNNY STACCATO was arbitrarily reduced from 3m 50s to 2m 31s, and there is no 7" version of DANCING IN THE DARK, which was an A-side (#37), but also *listed* as one of two supporting tracks on a 12" Single, though in the event the Album version was incorporated instead! See on #38 for details.

A-sides were thinner on the ground, as one would expect with a licenced collection at a budget price: MOZART FORTE, TELSTAR, IMAGINE: WOMAN, THEME FROM MISSING, DIAMONDS, MOUNTAINS OF THE MOON.

A must for completists, naturally, but the holding over of the individual issue *Dancing In The Dark* did induce some less avid collectors to lash out prematurely on the box, so acquiring two copies of the first two releases in the process (and ending up in many cases with five nasty brown discs, see on #57).

Nottingham 1990
Photograph: John Hank Humphrey

1990

#63

• Overseas LP/ CD,
Telstar STAR 2415 ~ ADE 395 // TCD2415 ~ ADE 660:
The Shadows At Their Very Best

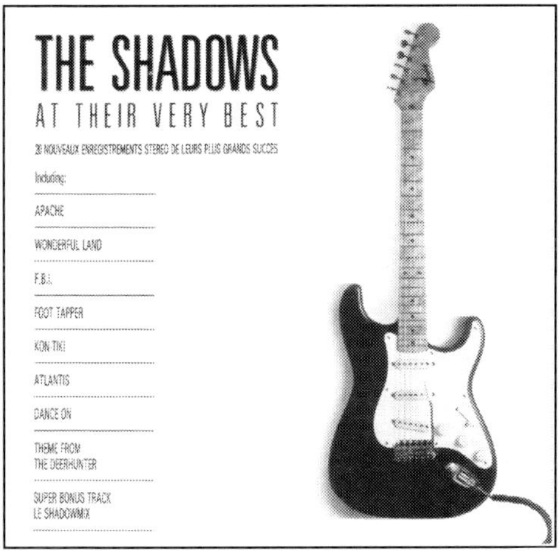

CD Running Time
56m 10s

Issued in France (a "TV Disc"). As the UK Album (#56), but with an extra track at the close: SHADOWMIX[82] (#55), a reasonable enough appendage given that the medley was a brew of the remakes.

82 For those who like to savour the riches of the French language, the front cover proclaims: "Super Bonus Track Le Shadowmix".

Usk 29 September 1990
Photographs: David Hawley

Bristol 22 October 1990
Photographs: David Hawley

Usk 29 September 1990
Photograph: David Hawley

Usk 29 September 1990
Photograph: David Hawley

Usk 29 September 1990
Photograph: David Hawley

Lakeside 3 October 1990
Photograph: David Hawley

Sheffield 1990
Photograph: John Hank Humphrey

Oxford 27 November 1990
Photograph: David Hawley

Croydon 18 October 1990
Photograph: David Hawley

Nottingham / Sheffield 1990
Photographs: John Hank Humphrey

Usk 29 September 1990
Photographs: David Hawley

1991

February 1991

#64

• CD, Pickwick PWKS 4031 P:
Dancing In The Dark

DANCING IN THE DARK[F] / LIFE IN THE JUNGLE[C] / QUEEN OF HEARTS[D] / CAT 'N' MOUSE[C] / I WILL RETURN[E] / SHOBA[G] / NO DANCING![C] / HIGH NOON[C] / TELSTAR[B] / MORE THAN I CAN SAY[B] / OUTDIGO[A] / SPOT THE BALL[H] / TIME IS TIGHT[D] / ELEVENIS[H] / MOUNTAINS OF THE MOON[G] / A WHITER SHADE OF PALE[D]

Note
The Disc itself carries the date 1989 (!)

Vocal Tracks
None

Distribution
UK

Running Time
60m 20s

****

The third 16-track Pickwick CD (no vinyl equivalent this time round) to offer selections from The Shadows' Polydor output (see #57, 60) drew on LP material from 1980 through to 1989, the compiler obviously having been given a fair degree of latitude: one track from *Change Of Address* (= A), two from *Hits Right Up Your Street* (B), four from *Life In The Jungle* (C), three from *The Silver Album/ XXV* (D), one from *Guardian Angel* (E), one from *Moonlight Shadows* (F), two from *Steppin' To The Shadows* (G), together with a couple of B-sides from 1982/83 (H: #12, #18). Of these, OUTDIGO from *Change Of Address* and the B-sides were new to CD.

Eight original compositions were included, making this the most varied and adventurous of the three Pickwick compilations (cf. Alan Taylor, *Pipeline* 8 [1991] 17).

This single CD had been marketed as part of a 3CD Box Set, see on #62 for an overview.

November 1991

#65

• LP/ CD, Polydor 511 374–1 // 511 374–2:
Themes And Dreams

CROCKETT'S THEME[H] / UP WHERE WE BELONG[C] / TAKE MY BREATH AWAY[E] / THEME FROM THE DEER HUNTER[G] / WALKING IN THE AIR[E] / IF YOU LEAVE ME NOW[A] / ONE DAY I'LL FLY AWAY[B] / AFRICA[C] // EVERY BREATH YOU TAKE[D] / MEMORY[C] / NIGHTS IN WHITE SATIN[D] / CANDLE IN THE WIND[F] / YOU WIN AGAIN[F] / SAILING[B] / JUST THE WAY YOU ARE[A] / MOONLIGHT SHADOW[D]

Vocal Tracks
None

UK Chart Performance

Date of first chart entry:	16 November 1991
Highest position in chart:	*21*
Weeks in chart:	11

Distribution: LP
UK, and Italy

Distribution: CD
UK, and Italy, Ukraine

CD Running Time
64m 51s

****

With no more fresh Albums to come, Polydor started to recycle the fruits of the previous decade. This 16–track Album takes in material from eight different sources: two tracks from *Change Of Address* (A), two from *Hits Right Up Your Street* (B), three from *The Silver Album/ XXV* (C), three from *Moonlight Shadows* (D), two from *Simply ... Shadows* (E), two from *Steppin' To The Shadows* (F), one from *The Shadows At Their Very Best* (G), one from *Reflection* (H).

On the whole (as the title suggests), this is The Shadows in relaxed, "easy-listening" mode, though some livelier moments are provided by memories of Jan Hammer, Toto, Sting, The Bee Gees and Mike Oldfield. Polydor's marketing instincts proved sound: this collection of chart-related cover versions, every one of them previously released, almost made the Top Twenty.

November 1991

#66

• CD / LP,
Reader's Digest 6-disc set RDCD 301-306 (~ 8 LP set GSHAD–A–219):
The Shadows Collection

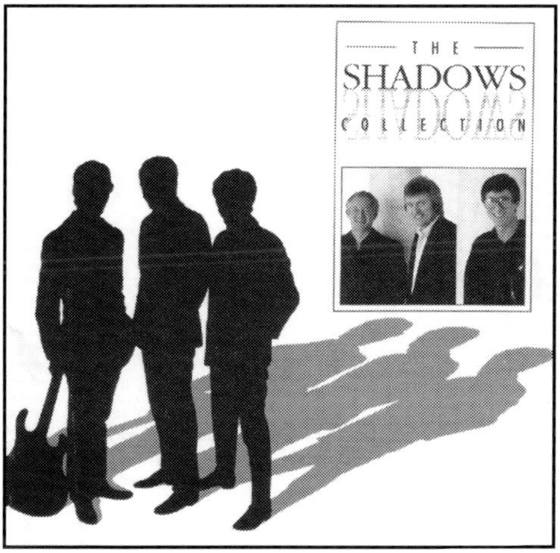

Track Listing

* Denotes Polydor tracks

Note The CD issue is set out here; for the layout over the 8LPs see Bernard Broche's *Discography 1958–2000*, under "LPs — 41/42".

Disc 1 [Polydor x 2, EMI x 20] (62m 29s)
APACHE / FOOT TAPPER / FBI / THE FRIGHTENED CITY / GERONIMO / KON-TIKI / MAN OF MYSTERY / WONDERFUL LAND / THE SAVAGE / GUITAR TANGO / DANCE ON! / ATLANTIS / SHINDIG / THE RISE AND FALL OF FLINGEL BUNT / DON'T MAKE MY BABY BLUE / GENIE WITH THE LIGHT BROWN LAMP / LET ME BE THE ONE / RIDERS IN THE SKY / A WHITER SHADE OF PALE*[D] / YOU DON'T HAVE TO SAY YOU LOVE ME*[D] / GOOD VIBRATIONS / PAPERBACK WRITER

Disc 2 [Polydor x 10, EMI x 6] (61m 24s)
GET BACK / PROUD MARY / IMAGINE : WOMAN*[B] / GOODBYE YELLOW BRICK ROAD / BRIDGE OVER TROUBLED WATER / SAILING*[B] / HEY JUDE*[E] / CLASSICAL GAS / JUST THE WAY YOU ARE*[A] / LET IT BE ME / MORE THAN I CAN SAY*[B] / ONE DAY I'LL FLY AWAY*[B] / WE DON'T TALK ANYMORE*[B] / THE POWER OF LOVE*[E] / THREE TIMES A LADY*[E] / HELLO*[E]

Disc 3 [Polydor x 8, EMI x 11] (62m 29s)
TAKE MY BREATH AWAY*[F] / IF YOU LEAVE ME NOW*[A] / ALL I ASK OF YOU*[G] / DON'T CRY FOR ME ARGENTINA / RIVER DEEP, MOUNTAIN HIGH / LUCILLE / HONKY TONK WOMEN / WALK DON'T RUN / BONY MORONIE / NUT ROCKER*[B] / TELSTAR*[B] / DIAMONDS*[D] / BLACK IS BLACK / WHAT'D I SAY / (I CAN'T GET NO) SATISFACTION / JOHNNY B GOODE / CATHY'S CLOWN / THIS OLE HOUSE*[B] / YOU KEEP ME HANGIN' ON*[G]

Disc 4 [Polydor x 8, EMI x 9] (63m 25s)
THE THIRD MAN*[B] / CHARIOTS OF FIRE*[C] / HIGH NOON*[C] / {MIDNIGHT COWBOY [Hank Marvin]} / THEMES FROM EASTENDERS & HOWARD'S WAY*[F] / CHI MAI*[B] / GOING HOME*[D] / PINBALL WIZARD : SEE ME FEEL ME / WALKING IN THE AIR*[F] / THEME FROM THE DEER HUNTER / BRIGHT EYES / UP WHERE WE BELONG*[D] / YOU'RE THE ONE THAT I WANT / BAKER STREET / SUPERSTAR / SAN FRANCISCO / SEMI-DETACHED SUBURBAN MR JAMES / LAST TRAIN TO CLARKSVILLE

Disc 5 [Polydor x 6, EMI x 15] (61m 48s)
WINCHESTER CATHEDRAL / THE MOST BEAUTIFUL GIRL / FRIDAY ON MY MIND / THE LETTER / HE AIN'T HEAVY, HE'S MY BROTHER*[G] / CANDLE IN THE WIND*[G] / SOMETHING'S GOTTEN HOLD OF MY HEART*[H] / TIME IS TIGHT*[D] / QUEEN OF HEARTS*[D] / MISTY*[B] / TONIGHT / STARDUST / IN THE MOOD / TEMPTATION / PERFIDIA / MARIA ELENA / DEEP PURPLE / BRAZIL / CHATTANOOGA CHOO-CHOO / THE LONELY BULL / SOUTH OF THE BORDER

Disc 6 [Polydor x 11, EMI x 5] (61m 05s)
FLY ME TO THE MOON / A LITTLE BITTY TEAR / TRAINS AND BOATS AND PLANES / GOD ONLY KNOWS / NIGHTS IN WHITE SATIN*[E] / I JUST CALLED TO SAY I LOVE YOU*[E] / MEMORY*[D] / THE LADY IN RED*[F] / CARELESS WHISPER*[F] / EQUINOXE (PART V)*[A] / AFRICA*[D] / EVERY BREATH YOU TAKE*[E] / HEART OF GLASS / MOONLIGHT SHADOW*[E] / THE WINNER TAKES IT ALL*[B] / I KNOW HIM SO WELL*[E]

Vocals (among Polydor tracks)
None

Distribution
UK

****

This bumper concentration of 111 tracks (112 actually: but one is credited to Hank Marvin) draws on EMI (66 tracks) and Polydor (45 tracks) material. All the Polydor tracks are cover versions, no group-compositions being included; they are drawn from eight different Albums, as follows:

• *Change Of Address*	3 tracks	= A
• *Hits Right Up Your Street*	12 tracks	= B
• *Life In The Jungle*	2 tracks	= C
• *The Silver Album/ XXV*	9 tracks	= D
• *Moonlight Shadows*	9 tracks	= E
• *Simply … Shadows*	5 tracks	= F
• *Steppin' To The Shadows*	4 tracks	= G
• *Reflection*	1 track	= H

Hits Right Up Your Street is thus the main source of supply: in fact, the twelve tracks on this set represent *all* the cover versions on that Album, the four originals not coming into the picture. It is essentially the same with *The Silver Album*: nine of the ten novel tracks on that reappear here, the tenth, a group-penned number (SHADOOGIE '83) being set aside.

The 6 CDs (as so often with RD products) are themed, rather untidily and not always aptly: details in *CD Guide* 102. There is a booklet with several pages of annotation, the author of which, amazingly, is not identified.

1992

May 1992

#67

CD, Polydor 813 574–2 ~ POL 899:
Change Of Address

Running Time
48m 10s

CD issue (UK) of 1980 LP, see #2. This one had been a long time coming, but not a lot of effort was put into it. There was only a single-page front insert (like the products of doubtful pedigree in cheap stores), which did not even trouble to take over from the LP details of personnel, recording venue and production.

May 1992

#68

• CD, Pickwick PWKS 4106:
Hits Right Up Your Street

Running Time
55m 11s

Budget reissue (UK) of 1987 Polydor CD, see #12. On offer here was bright new artwork (front and back cover) with a couple of pages of annotation which concluded with the justified boast "as eminently listenable as it was when first issued".

September 1992

#69

• CD, Pickwick PWKS 4134:
Life In The Jungle

Running Time
45m 34s

Budget reissue (UK) of 1989 Polydor CD, see #52. Another new-look release (see previous entry), this time with positively dazzling artwork.

September 1992

#70

• 3 CD/ 3 LP, Polydor (Polytel[83]) 513 449–2 // 513 449–1:
The Shadows: Complete

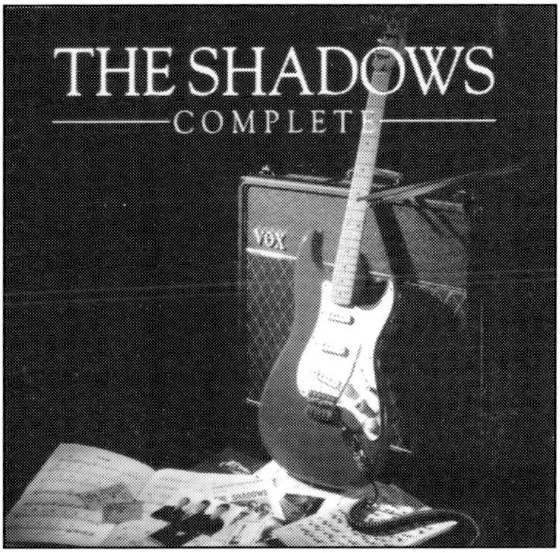

Note
The unlabelled tracks are all sourced from Album *The Shadows At Their Very Best;* in addition, in early pressings of the set *all three discs* bore the title 'The Classic Hits'

Disc 1/ Record 1 'The Classic Hits' (59m 05s)
APACHE / MAN OF MYSTERY / SHINDIG / KON-TIKI / WONDERFUL LAND / THE RISE AND FALL OF FLINGEL BUNT / THE BOYS / THE FRIGHTENED CITY / THE SAVAGE / THEME FOR YOUNG LOVERS / DANCE ON! / SHADOOGIE '83[D] // FBI / GUITAR TANGO / GENIE WITH THE LIGHT BROWN LAMP / ATLANTIS / FOOT TAPPER / GERONIMO / THE STRANGER / DON'T CRY FOR ME ARGENTINA / THEME FROM THE DEER HUNTER / RIDERS IN THE SKY '90[I]

Disc 2/ Record 2 'Shadows In The Moonlight' (68m 58s)
MOONLIGHT SHADOW[F] / THE LADY IN RED[G] / CROCKETT'S THEME[I] / TIME IS TIGHT[D] / YOU WIN AGAIN[H] / EVERY BREATH YOU TAKE[F] / ALL I ASK OF YOU[H] / CHI MAI[B] / MIDNIGHT CREEPIN'[A] // THE MUSIC OF THE NIGHT[G] / THREE TIMES A LADY[F] / RIGHT HERE WAITING[I] / THEME FROM MISSING[C] / GOING HOME[D] / EQUINOXE (PART V)[A] / DANCING IN THE DARK[F] / HELLO MR W.A.M.[A]

[83] Polytel: the television marketing arm of PolyGram.

Disc 3/ Record 3 'Original Shadows' (75m 08s)
PULASKI[G] / SUMMER LOVE '59[B] / COWBOY CAFE[B] / MOUNTAINS OF THE MOON[H] / STACK-IT[H] / THING-ME-JIG[B] / HATS OFF TO WALLY[B] / LIFE IN THE JUNGLE[C] / LOOK BACK ON LOVE[E] / NO DANCING![C] // THE OLD ROMANTICS[C] / SPOT THE BALL[J] / SHOBA[H] / CAT 'N' MOUSE[C] / JOHNNY STACCATO[E] / TURNING POINT[E] / THE SHADY LADY[J] / THE FOURTH MAN[J] / FENDER BENDER[J] / CHANGE OF ADDRESS[A]

• "Digital sound engineering by Gary Moore — Polygram, London"

Vocal Tracks
None

Distribution
UK

This "themed" (mail-order) set is the most substantial Polydor compilation to date, at 59 tracks. All 20 of the numbers on *The Shadows At Their Very Best* (#56) are included under the label 'The Classic Hits' — and so they are, in name at least. Two further tracks on Disc 1, and Discs 2–3 are put together from nine Albums, together with B-sides, as follows:

• *Change Of Address*	4 tracks	= A
• *Hits Right Up Your Street*	5 tracks	= B
• *Life In The Jungle*	5 tracks	= C
• *The Silver Album/ XXV*	3 tracks	= D
• *Guardian Angel*	3 tracks	= E
• *Moonlight Shadows*	4 tracks	= F
• *Simply ... Shadows*	3 tracks	= G
• *Steppin' To The Shadows*	5 tracks	= H
• *Reflection*	3 tracks	= I
• B-sides x 4	#1, 6, 12, 13	= J

Disc 3 provided a welcome move away from cover versions by offering a generous supply of group originals — but MIDNIGHT CREEPIN' on Disc 2 is in the wrong place. Another original (SHADOOGIE '83, on Disc 1) was making its debut on CD (see on #19 above). — JOHNNY STACCATO is the slimmed-down version already given an airing on Pickwick's *The Shadows Collection* (#57).

On the B-sides included see *CD Guide* 265.

1993

May 1993

#71

• CD, Polydor 843 798–2:
Shadows In The Night

THE LADY IN RED[D] / LOVE CHANGES EVERYTHING[F] / THE POWER OF LOVE[C] / THE WINNER TAKES IT ALL[A] / SEALED WITH A KISS[F] / ALL I ASK OF YOU[E] / ONE MOMENT IN TIME[E] / CARELESS WHISPER[D] / I JUST CALLED TO SAY I LOVE YOU[C] / I WANT TO KNOW WHAT LOVE IS[D] / I GUESS THAT'S WHY THEY CALL IT THE BLUES[D] / THEME FROM MISSING[B] / GOING HOME [Edit][G] / RIGHT HERE WAITING[F] / CHI MAI[A] / DANCING IN THE DARK[C]

Running Time
63m 49s

Vocal Tracks
None

UK Chart Performance

Date of first chart entry:	15 May 1993
Highest position in chart:	*22*
Weeks in chart:	4

Distribution
UK

****

Themes And Dreams (#65) sold pretty well in 1991/92, so it must have seemed natural to follow it up with another selection of tranquil, easy-going covers — with the odd burst of animation, notably in this case from the closing number.

The sources for this 16-tracker are:

• *Hits Right Up Your Street*	2 tracks	= A
• *Life In The Jungle*	1 track	= B
• *Moonlight Shadows*	3 tracks	= C
• *Simply ... Shadows*	4 tracks	= D
• *Steppin' To The Shadows*	2 tracks	= E
• *Reflection*	3 tracks	= F

• Also (G):
Polydor shrewdly dangled before the keen CD collector the DJ Promo of GOING HOME (#22); DANCING IN THE DARK might also have been offered in the so far undigitised 7" Single or 12" Single version, or both, but it was not to be.[84]

[84] For some background detail to this see Jim Nugent in *Pipeline* 19 (1993) 47.

June 1993

#72

• CD, Spectrum 550 0702:
Steppin' To The Shadows

UK budget issue of Polydor original from May 1989, see #51; also released in 1996 with plain white back cover, plain silver disc and clear plastic tray.

October 1993

#73

• CD, Spectrum 550 094–2:
Dreamtime

IMAGINE : WOMAN[B] / THREE TIMES A LADY[D] / JUST THE WAY YOU ARE[A] / IF YOU LEAVE ME NOW[A] / UP WHERE WE BELONG[C] / MISTY[B] / CARELESS WHISPER[E] / I GUESS THAT'S WHY THEY CALL IT THE BLUES[E] / I JUST CALLED TO SAY I LOVE YOU[D] / ALWAYS ON MY MIND[F] / SEALED WITH A KISS[F] / WALKING IN THE AIR[E] / GOING HOME[C] / THE SKYE BOAT SONG[E]

Running Time
52m 09s

Vocal Tracks
None

Distribution
UK, and Australia, Germany, Japan
After *Themes And Dreams* (#65) and *Shadows In The Night* (#71), a budget Spectrum release (with 14 rather than 16 tracks) in similar vein, a chiefly easy-on-the-ear selection of cover versions.[85] The sources are these:

• *Change Of Address*	2 tracks	= A
• *Hits Right Up Your Street*	2 tracks	= B
• *The Silver Album/ XXV*	2 tracks	= C
• *Moonlight Shadows*	2 tracks	= D
• *Simply ... Shadows*	4 tracks	= E
• *Reflection*	2 tracks	= F

See for evaluation Jim Nugent in *Pipeline* 21 (1993/94) 52–53.

[85] Four tracks on *Dreamtime* had already been used on *Themes*, and a further four on *In The Night* (the latter also offering a variation on GOING HOME).

October 1993

#74

• CD, PolyGram Special Products / Avon Cosmetics PSPCD 299:
The Shadows

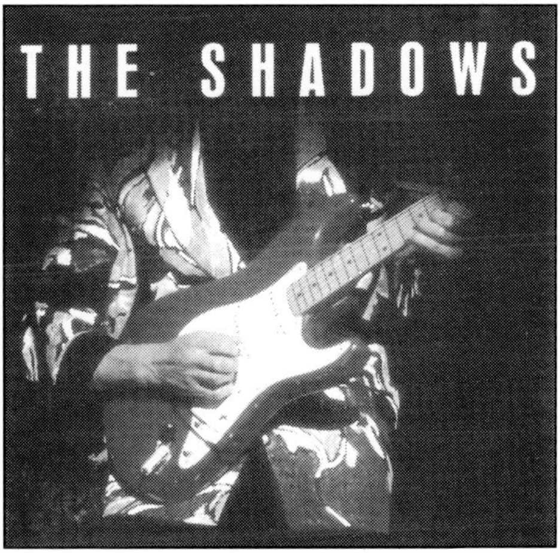

JUST THE WAY YOU ARE[A] / ALBATROSS[A] / SEALED WITH A KISS[E] / DIAMONDS[C] / A WHITER SHADE OF PALE[C] / WE DON'T TALK ANYMORE[B] / TELSTAR[B] / IMAGINE : WOMAN[B] / SOMETHING'S GOTTEN HOLD OF MY HEART[E] / THREE TIMES A LADY[D] / IF YOU LEAVE ME NOW[A] / TEMPTATION[A] / UPTOWN GIRL[E] / EQUINOXE (PART V)[A]

Running Time
54m 18s

Vocal Tracks
None

Distribution
UK

Another 14-track assemblage of cover versions, this one less accessible to the record-buying public; and rather less laid back than *Dreamtime* (see #73). Sources:

• *Change Of Address*	5 tracks	= A
• *Hits Right Up Your Street*	3 tracks	= B
• *The Silver Album/ XXV*	2 tracks	= C
• *Moonlight Shadows*	1 track	= D
• *Reflection*	3 tracks	= E

1993

#75

• Overseas 2CD, EMI 2505472 [+ reissue 1997, EMI 8310392]:
The Shadows Collection

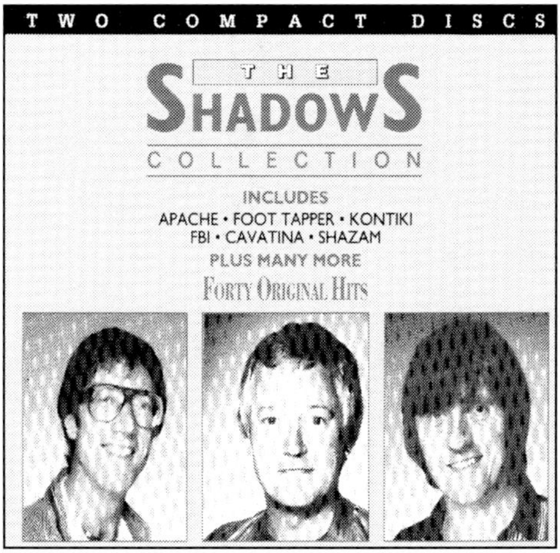

Running Time
49m 28s; 60m 15s

Issued in Australia. Disc 2 only of this set contains some Polydor material, corresponding to the New Zealand LP *20 Golden Greats Vol. 2* (1983, repressing), see on #23 above, and, on this set, also Ian Kershaw in *SCOFA* 32 (1993) 16.

1994

October 1994

#76

• CD, Polygram TV 523 821–2:
The Best Of Hank Marvin And The Shadows

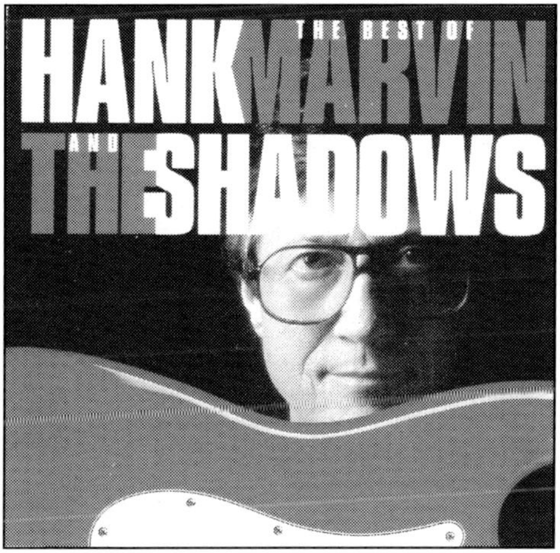

[* = Hank Marvin tracks]
ANOTHER DAY IN PARADISE* / EVERY BREATH YOU TAKE / JESSICA* / THE RISE AND FALL OF FLINGEL BUNT / ATLANTIS / I WILL ALWAYS LOVE YOU* / FOOT TAPPER / THEME FROM THE DEER HUNTER / HEARTBEAT* / (EVERYTHING I DO) I DO IT FOR YOU* / RIDERS IN THE SKY '90 / DANCE ON! / HOT ROX* / SYLVIA* / MOONLIGHT SHADOW / APACHE / MRS ROBINSON* / WALKING IN THE AIR / THE LADY IN RED / DON'T CRY FOR ME ARGENTINA / GUITAR TANGO / WONDERFUL LAND / KON-TIKI / FBI

Running Time
78m 44s

Vocal Tracks
None

UK Chart Performance

Date of first chart entry:	22 October 1994
Highest position in chart:	*19*
Weeks in chart:	11

Distribution
UK; see also #89 (reissue on Spectrum)

****

A return to the Top Twenty (with help from Christmas shoppers no doubt) for the first time since 1990 for this haphazard selection of twenty four tracks, sixteen by The Shadows, the rest by Hank Marvin. Included are eleven of the remade "classics" from *The Shadows At Their Very Best*, together with EVERY BREATH YOU TAKE and MOONLIGHT SHADOW from *Moonlight Shadows*, WALKING IN THE AIR (faded 5s early, so losing the arranged ending) and THE LADY IN RED from *Simply ... Shadows*, and RIDERS IN THE SKY '90 from *Reflection*. The emphasis throughout the set is on cover versions; there is a solitary exception, one lying outside the scope of this survey, Hank and Ben Marvin's composition HOT ROX.

1996

September 1996

#77

• CD, Spectrum 552 416–2:
Moonlight Shadows

UK budget issue of 1986 Polydor CD, see on #36 above. This time there was some brief annotation from Mark Brennan — a trifle lavish in its praise, as is often the way with commissions of this nature.

1997

November 1997

#78

• CD, PolyGram TV 539 479–2:
Hank Marvin And The Shadows
Play The Music Of
Andrew Lloyd Webber And Tim Rice

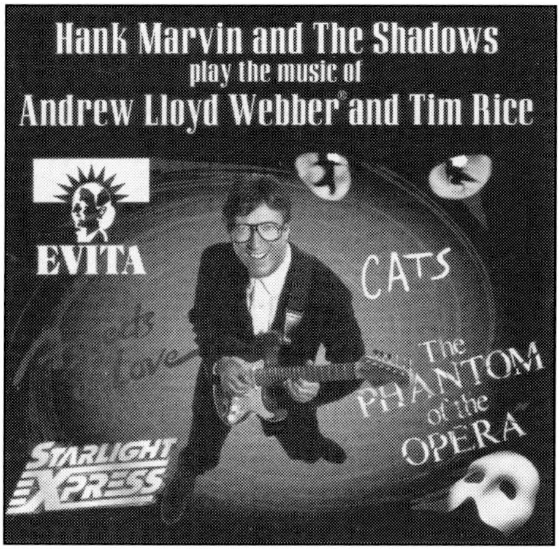

* = Shadows tracks
A WHOLE NEW WORLD / THE PHANTOM OF THE OPERA / MEMORY* / TELL ME ON A SUNDAY / I KNOW HIM SO WELL* / STARLIGHT EXPRESS SUITE / I'D BE SURPRISINGLY GOOD FOR YOU / DON'T CRY FOR ME ARGENTINA* / CAN YOU FEEL THE LOVE TONIGHT / LOVE CHANGES EVERYTHING* / OH WHAT A CIRCUS / THE MUSIC OF THE NIGHT* / TAKE THAT LOOK OFF YOUR FACE / ALL I ASK OF YOU* / ANOTHER SUITCASE IN ANOTHER HALL / ONE NIGHT IN BANGKOK — VARIATIONS

Running Time
73m 14s

Vocal Tracks
None

UK Chart Performance

Date of first chart entry:	22 November 1997
Highest position in chart:	*41*
Weeks in chart:	6

Distribution
UK

****

This was predominantly a showcase for Hank Marvin. The six Shadows' numbers were derived from *The Silver Album/ XXV* (MEMORY), *Moonlight Shadows* (I KNOW HIM SO WELL), *Simply ... Shadows* (THE MUSIC OF THE NIGHT), *Steppin' To The Shadows* (ALL I ASK OF YOU), *The Shadows At Their Very Best* (DON'T CRY FOR ME ARGENTINA), *Reflection* (LOVE CHANGES EVERYTHING). One of the most laid back Albums in the present survey, but this is not the place to evaluate it in its entirety (see *Shadsfax* 13 [1997] 15–17; *Pipeline* 38 [1998] 30–31).

1998

July 1998

#79

• CD, See For Miles SEECD 494:
Shadstrax

• Tracks sequenced by Bruce Welch

MOUNTAINS OF THE MOON[F] / SUMMER LOVE '59[B] / OUTDIGO[A] / COWBOY CAFE[B] / HATS OFF TO WALLY[B] / CAT 'N' MOUSE[C] / ELEVENIS[G] / TURNING POINT[E] / THE OLD ROMANTICS[C] / SPOT THE BALL[G] / FENDER BENDER[G] / CHANGE OF ADDRESS[A] / LIFE IN THE JUNGLE[C] / THE FOURTH MAN[G] / MIDNIGHT CREEPIN'[A] / THE SHADY LADY[G] / THING-ME-JIG[B] / STACK-IT [F]/ NO DANCING![C] / SHOBA[F] / SHADOOGIE '83[D]

Running Time
78m 41s

Vocal Tracks
None

Distribution
UK

****

The foremost point worth making about this collection is that it is superbly documented, with track-notes (for which certain group-members have been consulted) from Rob Bradford. It is not one of your usual purposeless compilations either: it consists "entirely of original Shadows' compositions recorded between 1980 and 1989".[86] Running time is generous: we can overlook the second clipped off SHOBA (hardly enough to give it AV status!).

The sources for the 21 tracks are as follows:

• *Change Of Address*	3 tracks	= A
• *Hits Right Up Your Street*	4 tracks	= B
• *Life In The Jungle*	4 tracks	= C
• *The Silver Album/ XXV*	1 track	= D
• *Guardian Angel*	1 track	= E
• *Steppin' To The Shadows*	3 tracks	= F
• B-sides (#1, 6, 12, 13, 18)	5 tracks	= G

All compositions by the principal group members during the stay at Polydor are represented, with these exceptions:

- From *Change Of Address*
  ARTY'S PARTY
- From *Life In The Jungle*
  The vocal YOU RESCUE ME[87]
- From *Guardian Angel*
  LOOK BACK ON LOVE, JOHNNY STACCATO, OUR ALBERT
- From *Simply ... Shadows*
  PULASKI

86 See also *CD Guide* 266.
87 A number originally marked out for inclusion on *Shadstrax*, see Tony Hoffman in *Shadsfax* 18 (1998) 5.

The three *Guardian Angel* tracks would be catered for by a further See For Miles release at the end of the year (#81). What a pity that the bonus tracks for that did not pick up the three residual pieces specified above and so parcel up the "originals" very neatly.

September 1998

#80

• 2 CD, PolyGram TV 559 211–2:
The Very Best Of Hank Marvin & The Shadows — The First 40 Years

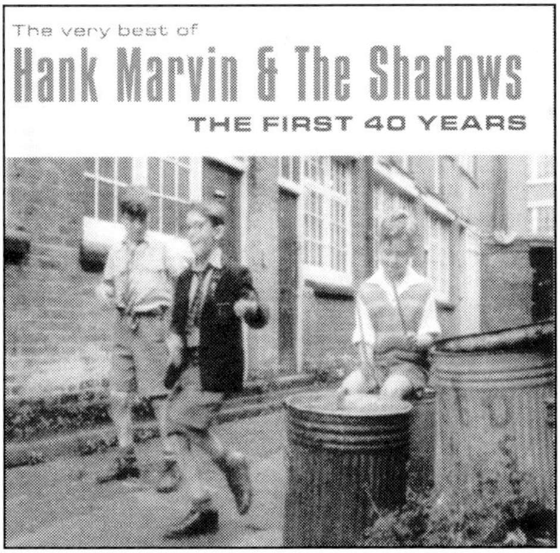

With ***Disc 2*** (19 tracks Hank Marvin) we are not concerned;

Disc 1 The Shadows
APACHE / THE RISE AND FALL OF FLINGEL BUNT / MAN OF MYSTERY / MOONLIGHT SHADOW / THEME FROM THE DEER HUNTER / THE SAVAGE / GUITAR TANGO / THE BOYS / WONDERFUL LAND / GERONIMO / MEMORY / GENIE WITH THE LIGHT BROWN LAMP / EVERY BREATH YOU TAKE / THE FRIGHTENED CITY / KON-TIKI / WALKING IN THE AIR / ATLANTIS / SHINDIG / THE LADY IN RED / DANCE ON! / DON'T CRY FOR ME ARGENTINA / THE STRANGER / THEME FOR YOUNG LOVERS / FOOT TAPPER / FBI / RIDERS IN THE SKY '90

• "Compilation mastered by Philip Soule at PolyGram Digital Studios"

Running Time
75m 21s; 77m 20s

Vocal Tracks
None

Distribution
UK

UK Chart Performance

Date of first chart entry:	14 November 1998
Highest position in chart:	*56*
Weeks in chart:	5

****

The "Very Best" of The Shadows on this reckoning is the collection of twenty remakes of the classic tracks (from *The Shadows At Their Very Best*), with half a dozen odds and ends thrown in to take the disc over the magic 74m mark: MEMORY from *The Silver Album/ XXV*, MOONLIGHT SHADOW and EVERY BREATH YOU TAKE from *Moonlight Shadows*, WALKING IN THE AIR and THE LADY IN RED from *Simply ... Shadows*, RIDERS IN THE SKY '90 from *Reflection*. A more judicious approach to *At Their Very Best* might have allowed room for a wider selection of other material more representative of their 80's output (cf. Tony Hoffman in *Shadsfax* 20 [1998] 4).

December 1998

#81

• CD, See For Miles SEECD 679:
Guardian Angel ... Plus

HOW DO I LOVE THEE / HAMMERHEAD / THE SATURDAY WESTERN / LOOK BACK ON LOVE / JOHNNY STACCATO / I WILL RETURN / (I'M GONNA BE YOUR) GUARDIAN ANGEL / CAN'T PLAY YOUR GAME / ON A NIGHT LIKE THIS / TURNING POINT / OUR ALBERT / — **Bonus tracks**: DANCING IN THE DARK (12" Remix) / INDIGO / THE MODERN WAY / LIVERPOOL DAYS / YOU DON'T HAVE TO SAY YOU LOVE ME / GOING HOME (DJ Edit) / TIME IS TIGHT / EQUINOXE (PART V) (Single Edit)

Running Time
79m 09s

Vocal Tracks
7, 8, 9, 14, 15

Distribution
UK

For the original *Guardian Angel* Album see on #27 above. — The extras (see also on #79): the most important are without doubt the newcomers to CD, the 12" Single version of DANCING IN THE DARK (#38) and the edited version of EQUINOXE (PART V) (#1). Then there are some rarities, INDIGO from *Change Of Address*, YOU DON'T HAVE TO SAY YOU LOVE ME and TIME IS TIGHT from *The Silver Album/ XXV*, THE MODERN WAY and LIVERPOOL DAYS from *XXV*, and finally the edit of GOING HOME (see #22) which had been transferred to CD on *Shadows In The Night* (#71).

As with CD *Shadstrax*, so with *Guardian Angel ... Plus* there is an exemplary set of track-notes from Rob Bradford. "All in all a great release to end the fortieth anniversary with", Tony Hoffman, *Shadsfax* 21 (1999) 11.

1998

#82

• Overseas CD, Karussel (Sanity) 552 416–2:
The Shadows. Collection Series

Running Time
66m 21s

Issued in Australia, Sanity being a chain of Aussie record shops. Content as for CD *Moonlight Shadows* (#36); with this issue there are a couple of pages of liner notes from Mark Brennan, as was the case with the 1996 budget *Moonlight* (and its 1998 Australian derivative). What on earth is John Rostill doing on the sleeve of this one?

1998

#83

• Overseas CD, PolyGram Special Products MMTCD 2011:
The Ballads

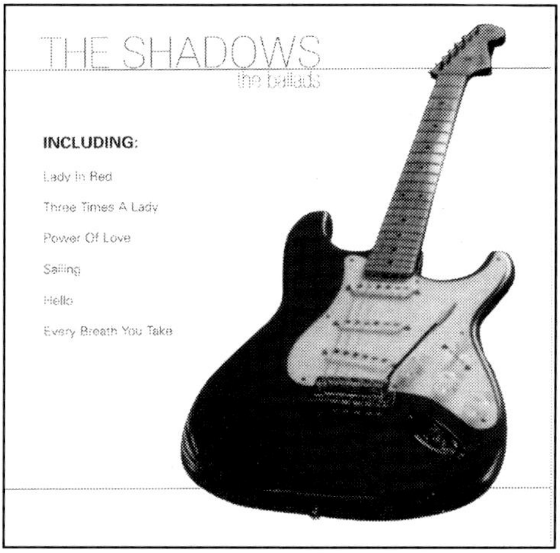

THE POWER OF LOVE[A] / CARELESS WHISPER[B] / THE LADY IN RED[B] / I WANT TO KNOW WHAT LOVE IS [B] / HELLO[A] / I JUST CALLED TO SAY I LOVE YOU[A] / THREE TIMES A LADY[A] / MEMORY[A] / TAKE MY BREATH AWAY[B] / AGAINST ALL ODDS[A] / I KNOW HIM SO WELL[A] / JEALOUS GUY[B] / NIGHTS IN WHITE SATIN[A] / A WHITER SHADE OF PALE[A] / SAILING[A] / IMAGINE: WOMAN[A]

Running Time
68m 31s

Vocal Tracks
None

Issued in South Africa, a compilation by Chris Venter. Eleven tracks from *Moonlight Shadows*, five from *Simply ... Shadows*. OK, I'm cheating here a bit, because two of the Moonlighters had appeared on *Hits Right Up Your Street*, and two on *The Silver Album/ XXV*. Just to show aspiring compilers how these things can be put together with practically no effort so long as you don't doze off in the process.

Still, there was obviously some lively (?) debate about what to call the finished product: *The Ballads* front cover / disc, *The Ballad Collection* spine. But nobody could think of anything to say on the back cover of the front insert.

1998

#84

• Overseas CD, PolyGram TV 559 126–2:
Master Series — The Shadows

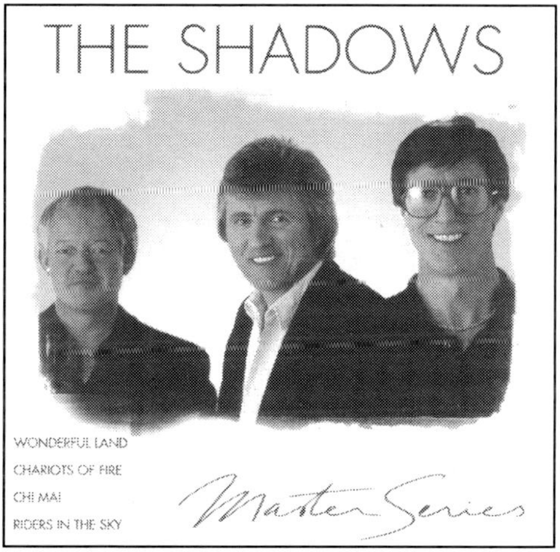

MOUNTAINS OF THE MOON[F] / WONDERFUL LAND[G] / A WHITER SHADE OF PALE[C] / WALK OF LIFE[D] / WE DON'T NEED ANOTHER HERO[E] / DANCE ON![G] / HEAVEN IS A PLACE ON EARTH[F] / GUITAR TANGO[G] / DANCING IN THE DARK[D] / STRAWBERRY FIELDS FOREVER[H] / CHARIOTS OF FIRE[B] / CHAIN

REACTION[E] / CHI MAI[A] / THE THIRD MAN[A] / THEME FROM MISSING[B] / ONE MOMENT IN TIME[F] / THE MUSIC OF THE NIGHT[E] / RIDERS IN THE SKY '90[H]

Running Time
70m 37s

Vocal Tracks
None

Distribution
Austria, France, Germany, Switzerland

****

An 18-track assortment, sourced as follows:

• *Hits Right Up Your Street*	2 tracks	= A
• *Life In The Jungle*	2 tracks	= B
• *The Silver Album/ XXV*	1 track	= C
• *Moonlight Shadows*	2 tracks	= D
• *Simply ... Shadows*	3 tracks	= E
• *Steppin' To The Shadows*	3 tracks	= F
• *The Shadows At Their Very Best*	3 tracks	= G
• *Reflection*	2 tracks	= H

On the menu therefore: four Shadows' remakes[88] (including RIDERS IN THE SKY from *Reflection*), one original (MOUNTAINS OF THE MOON), and a selection of chart-related[89] cover versions, together with their own chart candidate THE THIRD MAN.

[88] On what principle (if any) these particular tracks were picked upon we shall never know; perhaps it is as well that such things generally remain dark.
[89] THEME FROM MISSING came into this category belatedly, as a track on Vangelis' Album *Themes* (1989): see on #14.

1998

#85

• Overseas CD, Rotation Polymedia 554 744–2:
One Moment In Time

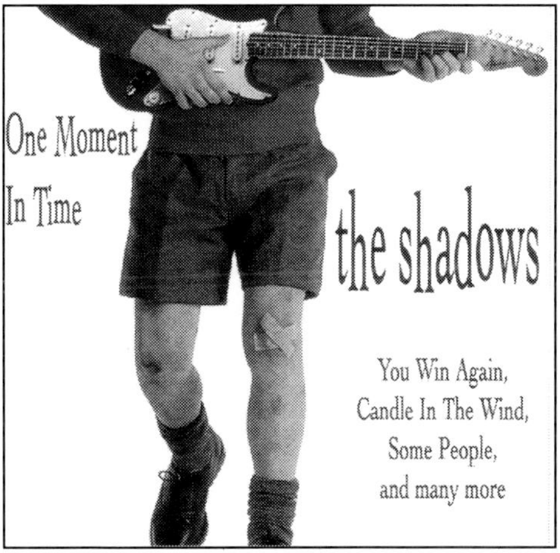

Running Time
69m 02s

Issued in Holland. Content as *Steppin' To The Shadows*, see #51.

1999

April 1999

#86

• CD, Spectrum 554 874–2:
Simply ... Shadows

Budget reissue of Polydor CD, see #44.

1999

#87

• Overseas 5CD Box Set, EMI 7243 4 96561 2 3:
The Shadows Complete

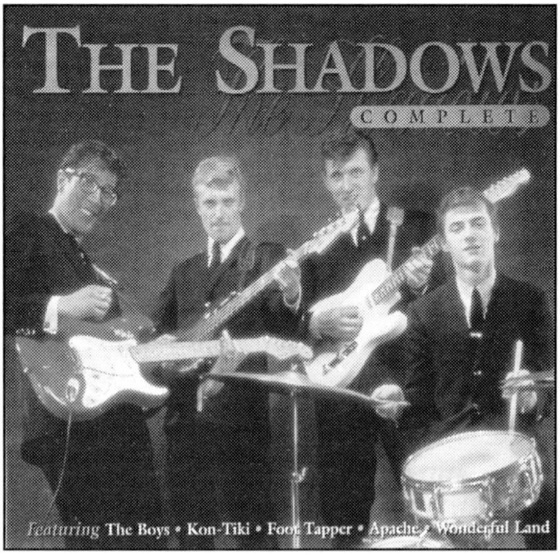

There are 100 tracks on this Australian issue, 96 by The Shadows, but only 18 drawing upon our Polydor material:

Disc 3 ('Let's Rock')
THIS OLE HOUSE[B]

Disc 4 ('Big Hits — Shadows' Style')
ALBATROSS[A] / CHARIOTS OF FIRE[C]

Disc 5 ('The 80s and [since Hank Marvin is included] 90s')
CHAIN REACTION[F] / FLASHDANCE ... WHAT A FEELING[H] / SOME PEOPLE[G] / THEMES FROM EASTENDERS & HOWARD'S WAY[F] / CHI MAI[B] / ALL I ASK OF YOU[G] / THE MUSIC OF THE NIGHT[F] / MEMORY[D] / CANDLE IN THE WIND[G] / MOONLIGHT SHADOW[E] / CROCKETT'S THEME[H] / ALWAYS ON MY MIND[H] / THE LADY IN RED[F] / ONE MOMENT IN TIME[G] / I WANNA DANCE WITH SOMEBODY[G]

An assortment of cover versions, sourced from these Albums:

• *Change Of Address*	1 track	= A
• *Hits Right Up Your Street*	2 tracks	= B
• *Life In The Jungle*	1 track	= C
• *The Silver Album/ XXV*	1 track	= D
• *Moonlight Shadows*	1 track	= E
• *Simply ... Shadows*	4 tracks	= F
• *Steppin' To The Shadows*	5 tracks	= G
• *Reflection*	3 tracks	= H

Booklets are provided for all five discs (annotation by Bruce Ward).

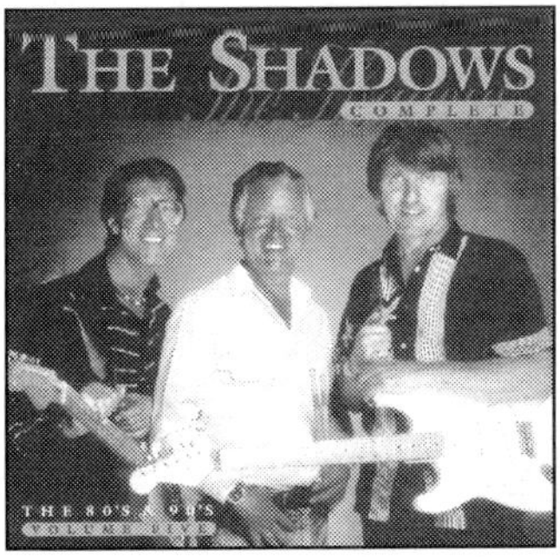

The last of the five CDs has a Polydor-era front pic.

2000

July 2000

#88

• 2 CD, EMI 7243 5 27586 2 3:
50 Golden Greats

UK Chart Performance

Date of first chart entry:	12 August 2000
Highest position in chart:	*35*
Weeks in chart:	3

This UK release is essentially an EMI collection, a sort of expanded version of the celebrated *20 Golden Greats*, with half a dozen Polydor covers tacked on at the end of Disc 2 (and boasted about in the EMI blurb! — See *Shadsfax* 28 [1999] 9–10):

ALBATROSS from *Change Of Address*, IMAGINE: WOMAN from *Hits Right Up Your Street*, A WHITER SHADE OF PALE and MEMORY from *The Silver Album/ XXV*, NIGHTS IN WHITE SATIN from *Moonlight Shadows*; and, of all things, the Promo Edit of GOING HOME from 1983 (#22).

September 2000

#89

• CD, Spectrum 544 437–2:
The Best Of Hank Marvin & The Shadows

Budget reissue of PolyGram TV original, see #76.

2000

#90

• Overseas 2CD, EMI TOCP–65649–50:
Golden Greats

Japanese enlarged version of #88 (see *Shadsfax* 31 [2001] 3–4). The Polydor tracks are the same.

2001

March 2001

#91

• CD in two editions,
(1) Crimson CRIMCD 302; (ii) Music Club MCCD 452:
Hank Marvin & The Shadows — The Singles Collection

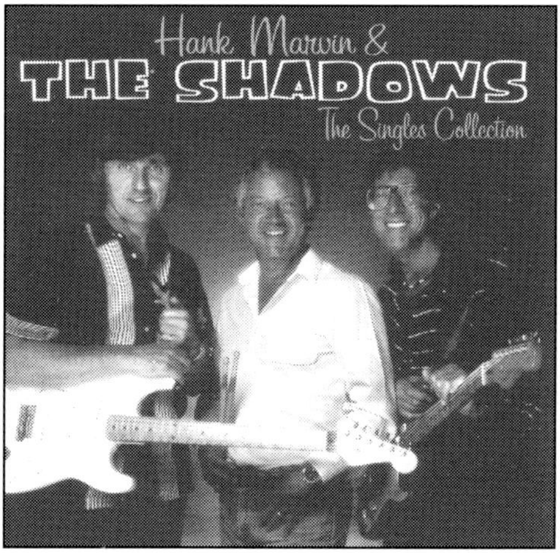

* = Hank Marvin tracks; ** featuring Brian May; *** featuring Mark Knopfler

EQUINOXE (PART V) / MOZART FORTE / THE THIRD MAN / TELSTAR / IMAGINE: WOMAN / DON'T TALK* / THE TROUBLE WITH ME IS YOU* / TREAT ME NICE / THE THEME FROM MISSING / THE HAWK AND THE DOVE* / INVISIBLE MAN* / DIAMONDS / GOING HOME / ON A NIGHT LIKE THIS [shortened] / MOONLIGHT SHADOW / DANCING IN THE DARK [7" AV! See below] / THE THEMES FROM EASTENDERS & HOWARD'S WAY / PULASKI / WALKING IN THE AIR [shortened] / MOUNTAINS OF THE MOON / SHADOWMIX / WE ARE THE CHAMPIONS** / WONDERFUL LAND***

Running Time
78m 45s

Distribution
UK

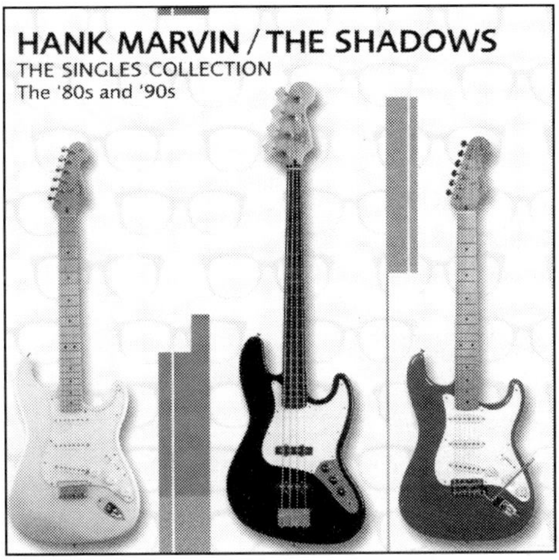

There are two different issues of this set, the Crimson (which lacks the sleeve-notes of the other) being targeted at Woolworths, Tesco and other chains. The idea, with The Shadows, is to provide an ordered sequence of UK Polydor A-Singles (EQUINOXE (PART V) and GOING HOME are the edits [#1, #22]).

All is not plain sailing however by any means: ON A NIGHT LIKE THIS has been drastically pruned, taken down from 3m 49s to 2m 33s, in order to fit everything in. A bit of a blemish. (See further *Shadsfax* 31 [2001] 6–8.)

In addition, WALKING IN THE AIR is faded (at 3m 43s; full version with an arranged ending 3m 50s).

Even more noteworthy, not to say remarkable, is the fact that the 7" version of DANCING IN THE DARK, though scheduled for (first CD) release here, has been mysteriously supplanted by an alternative version, the existence of which had not so much as been hinted at anywhere. Presumably a master containing a variant (or more than one variant??) of Murray Munro's remixing activities was archived at Polydor alongside the version actually released.

The deviations from the 7" relate to the drum parts (differences in or absence of) in the sequences 16s to 1m 07s and 1m 08s to 1m 14s respectively.[90]

May 2001

#92

CD, Universal / Connoisseur VSOP CD 341:
The Hit Sound Of The Shadows

APACHE / MAN OF MYSTERY / THE STRANGER / FBI / THE FRIGHTENED CITY / KON-TIKI / THE SAVAGE / WONDERFUL LAND / GUITAR TANGO / DANCE ON! / FOOT TAPPER / ATLANTIS / SHINDIG / GERONIMO / THEME FOR YOUNG LOVERS / THE RISE AND FALL OF FLINGEL BUNT / DON'T CRY FOR ME ARGENTINA / THEME FROM THE DEER HUNTER / RIDERS IN THE SKY '90 / THE THIRD MAN

Running Time
53m 30s

90 My thanks to Les Woosey for information and guidance on this point.

Distribution
UK

Eighteen of the twenty remakes in a budget issue from the full-price *The Shadows At Their Very Best* (#56). THE BOYS and GENIE WITH THE LIGHT BROWN LAMP are dropped, replaced by THE THIRD MAN from *Hits Right Up Your Street* and RIDERS IN THE SKY from *Reflection*. See further *Shadsfax* 34 [2001] 3. — Interesting annotation.

July 2001

#93

• 2CD, See For Miles SEECD 732:
Live At Abbey Road / Live At The Liverpool Empire

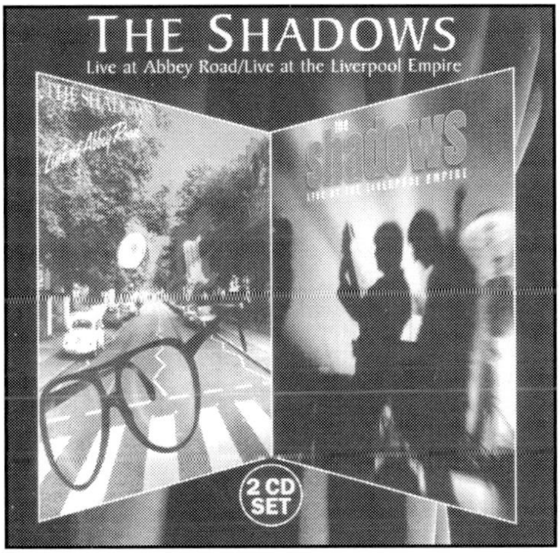

CD 1 (43m 11s)
Reissue of #53 (CD issue of #15)
CD 2 (54m 29s)
RIDERS IN THE SKY / THE STRANGER: KON-TIKI / ATLANTIS / THEME FROM THE DEER HUNTER / THE RISE AND FALL OF FLINGEL BUNT / TRUE LOVE WAYS / FOOT TAPPER / SHADOOGIE / TIME IS TIGHT / THE FRIGHTENED CITY / WONDERFUL LAND / DANCE ON! / CAPTAIN HADDOCK IS MISSING / APACHE / FBI

Vocal Track
6

Distribution
UK

A notable release, with excellent sleeve-notes by Rob Bradford and David Martin. The May 1989 issue of *Abbey Road* is no longer available. CD 2, drawn from a 1989 performance, was issued on *The Definitive Live Album*, no less: HQ Records HQ 06, Italy 1994 (see *CD Guide* 31, together with Jim Nugent, *Pipeline* 27 [1995] 35). However, the present disc is entirely legal and above board, and is in remastered form. Among the tracks included neither TRUE LOVE WAYS[91] (Buddy Holly/ Norman Petty) nor CAPTAIN HADDOCK IS MISSING (containing a lengthy drum solo from composer Brian Bennett) made it into the recording studio.

More on these sets in *Shadsfax* 33 [2001] 6–7; and from Alan Taylor, *Pipeline* 53 (2001) 45/47, who, hot on the heels of the Gretsch controversy, sets out to stir up another by asserting that he is "the 33rd handclap from the left on Brian's drum solo" at the Abbey Road session: only your ears can decide.

Pictured on next page:

The Definitive Live Album front cover, together with a single sheet insert which carries a track-listing and the Italian government's official "seal of approval". Not that this of course renders the release "legitimate" in any meaningful sense.

[91] Another "cover" to add to the mountain: a hit first for Buddy Holly, in 1960 (No. 25).

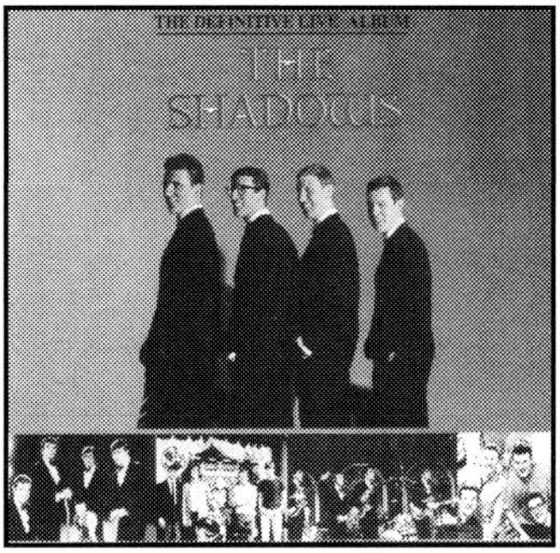

HQ 06

THE SHADOWS
THE DEFINITIVE LIVE ALBUM

1. GHOST RIDERS IN THE SKY
(Stan Jones) 3'38"

2. THE STRANGER
(Crompton/Jones) 3'58"

3. ATLANTIS
(Jerry Lordan) 3'01"

4. THEME FROM 'THE DEER HUNTER'
(Stanley Myers) 5'36"

5. THE RISE AND FALL OF FLINGLE BUNT
(B. Welch/H. Marvin/J. Rostill/B. Bennett) 3'13"

6. TRUE LOVE WAYS
(B. Holly/N. Petty) 3'20"

7. FOOT TAPPER
(H. Marvin/B. Welch//) 2'52"

8. SHADOOGIE
(H. Marvin/B. Welch/J. Harris/T. Meehan) 2'52"

9. TIME IS TIGHT
(Booker T. Jones) 4'37"

10. THE FRIGHTENED CITY,
(N. Paramor) 2'55"

11. WONDERFUL LAND
(Jerry Lordan) 2'28"

12. DANCE ON
(R. Adams/E. Murtagh) 2'33"

13. CAPTAIN HADDOCK IS MISSING
(B. Bennett) 7'36"

14. APACHE
(Jerry Lordan) 4'10"

15. F.B.I.
(Peter Gormley) 3'06"

2001

#94

• Overseas CD, EMI 7243 531809 2 8:
Kon-Tiki: de beste 1960–1980

Issued in Norway. This splendidly presented compilation has a claim on our attention because its final track (27) is the Polydor 7" edit of EQUINOXE (PART V) (#1 above).

2002

2002

#95

• Overseas CD, Disky (Pure Gold) GO 793402:
Guitar Tango

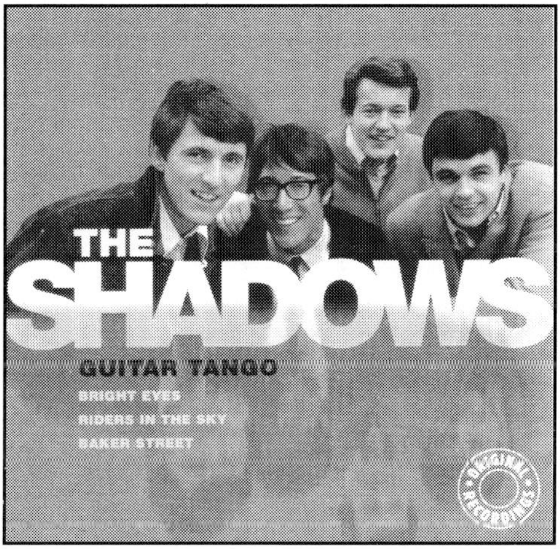

A Dutch release offering a single Polydor track, ALBATROSS (see #2).

2000

DVD #1

• EMI 07243 4 ~ 81232 9 9:
The Shadows Live

Recorded at The National Exhibition Centre, Birmingham (VHS Video release 1986):

SHADOOGIE / TIME IS TIGHT / THEME FROM THE DEER HUNTER / EQUINOXE (PART V) / WONDERFUL LAND / APACHE / FBI

Running Time
24m 55s

"A pathetic offering", Tony Hoffman, *Shadsfax* 29 [2000] 6 — certainly so in terms of presentation (par for the course with Shads' CDs generally speaking).

On the performance itself: of the original issue *The Rock Yearbook* Vol. VII (ed. Tom Hibbert, Virgin Books: London 1986) remarked: "A very restrained video, with a craftsman's approach to the material and a touchingly unhip light display during 'Apache'".

****

[A further DVD appeared in November 2002, which hardly merits inclusion in a serious discographical work: *Cliff Richard Plus The Shadows*, Classic Pictures DVD6080X: alongside two Cliff numbers supplemented by a diet of (amongst others) Alexis Korner, The Moody Blues, Placido Domingo and even "Bach" (you name it, it's in there somewhere), we are presented with The Shadows on German TV in 1981 against a background of around 4m of the edited version of EQUINOXE (PART V).]

APPENDIX

EMI COVER VERSIONS

While they were with EMI The Shadows (together with mentor Norrie Paramor in the early years) seemed by and large to have determined themselves what material to record, including in the process a significant number of their own compositions, through the 1960s especially.[1]

The change of label entailed a different approach: there was a marked decrease for one reason or another in original compositions, with correspondingly increasing emphasis on cover versions of chart hits, particularly hits which would be relatively fresh in the minds of the targeted audience.

Even so, it would be a mistake to suppose (as a casual glance at a Discography might suggest) that cover versions of this complexion (viz., chart-orientated covers) played a negligible part in the success story of The Shadows at EMI. Rather, at times the role of covers was pretty insignificant, while at other times this was far from being the case, as a rapid survey of Albums and Singles will show.[2]

---

[1] See the data accumulated in *CD Guide* 293–294.
[2] As it happens, EPs do not come into the picture. — "... covers have always played a great part in their recording career" remarks Jochen Bartsch in *SCOFA* 39 (1999) 9; I am with him there, but the percentage figures he goes on to offer for individual Albums are not especially illuminating: one needs to consider too the *nature* of the covers, rather than lumping together everything not composed within the group in one undifferentiated mass.

A. ALBUMS

Jigsaw in 1967 with its high proportion of cover versions marked something of a departure for The Shadows. Prior to that very little account was taken of recently successful chart material.

On *The Shadows* from 1961, **BLUE STAR** was somewhat remote in chart terms, a hit in 1955 for various artists both in the UK and the USA. On the other hand, **BABY MY HEART** had been a No. 33 for The Crickets as recently as 1960, while Santo and Johnny had made No. 22 with **SLEEPWALK** in 1959 (a USA No. 1, and already thoroughly well known among the instrumental fraternity, who seemed particularly adept at identifying "classics" early on!).

The second Album, *Out Of The Shadows* (1962) only brought a rendition of the "standard" **PERFIDIA**, a fairly recent No. 4 (No. 15 in the USA) for The Ventures, in 1960/61 (though The Shadows' version is radically different).

On *Dance With The Shadows* (1964) some at least of the following may have been suggested by specific chart entrants: **ZAMBESI** (Lou Busch & His Orchestra, No. 2 in 1956[3]); **IN THE MOOD** (Ernie Fields Orchestra, UK No. 13/ USA No. 4 in 1959[4]); **TEMPTATION** (The Everly Brothers, UK No. 1/ USA No. 27 in 1961[5]); **TONIGHT** (Shirley Bassey UK No. 21 in 1962; also as instr. Ferrante & Teicher, USA No. 8 in 1961); **CHATTANOOGA CHOO-CHOO** (Floyd Cramer, USA No. 36 in 1962); **THE LONELY BULL** (Herb Alpert & His Tijuana Brass, UK No. 22 in 1963/ USA No. 6 in 1962). However, as Les Woosey pertinently adds, "The Shadows in their formative years would have clearly been as much influenced by the preferences of Norrie Paramor. He was a skilled arranger, composer and conductor with a vast store of musical knowledge and experience from prior decades. Hence, I don't think Shirley Bassey or Floyd Cramer would have been a model half as much as the 1961 musical film or those big bands of the Forties".

---

3 A lesser entrant that same year was trumpeter Eddie Calvert: on his version of ZAMBESI he was accompanied by Norrie Paramor's orchestra.
4 However, the direct model, as Jim Nugent points out to me, was certainly Joe Loss' 'Twistin' The Mood' (B-side HMV POP959, 1961; also on EP *Twistin' At The Palais*, HMV 7EG 8749, 1962: see Trev Faull, *60's Brit-Pop Instrumentals* 212). I suspect that Joe Loss was the main inspiration (via Norrie Paramor) behind other "big-band" adaptations from around this period.
5 One wonders whether The Shadows had any knowledge of the Jet & Tony-styled version by Columbia stablemate Bobby Taylor, released in 1964 (DB 7282), now accessible on CD Stylus 10 PTING 1, track 27.

The Sound Of The Shadows (1965) offers, in addition to another Everly Brothers' number, **LET IT BE ME** (UK No. 13/ USA No. 7 in 1960[6]), Burl Ives' **A LITTLE BITTY TEAR** (UK/USA No. 9 in 1962; Miki & Griff UK No. 16) and **DEEP PURPLE** from Nino Tempo & April Stevens (UK No. 17/ USA No. 1 in 1963).

Shadow Music (1966) is virtually cover-free: the inclusion of **FLY ME TO THE MOON** may have owed something to acquaintance with Joe Harnell's distinctive 'Fly Me To The Moon — Bossa Nova' of 1963 (USA No. 14).

We now come to *Jigsaw* (1967), highlighted at the outset of this survey. The Everly Brothers are represented yet again, with the superlative **CATHY'S CLOWN** (UK/ USA No. 1 in 1960); but this is only the first of a number of 60's hits featured here. The oldie **TENNESSEE WALTZ** was taken to No. 35 in the USA by Sam Cooke in 1964; **STARDUST** to No. 32 in the USA by Nino Tempo & April Stevens that same year; **MARIA ELENA** to No. 6 in the USA (No. 5 in the UK) by Los Indios Tabajaras in 1963. Even more recent hits were:

• From 1965: **TRAINS AND BOATS AND PLANES**: Burt Bacharach & Orchestra (No. 4) and Billy J Kramer & The Dakotas (No. 12).

• From 1966: **SEMI-DETACHED SUBURBAN MR JAMES**: Manfred Mann (No. 2); **FRIDAY ON MY MIND** The Easybeats (No. 6/ USA No. 16 in 1967); **WINCHESTER CATHEDRAL** The New Vaudeville Band (No. 4/ No. 1 USA).

From Hank, Bruce, Brian & John (1967 again) maintained this trend:

• From 1966: **HOLY COW** Lee Dorsey (No. 6/ USA No. 23)

• From 1967: **SAN FRANCISCO** Scott McKenzie (No. 1/ USA No. 4); **THE LETTER** The Box Tops (No. 5/ USA No. 1); **LAST TRAIN TO CLARKSVILLE** The Monkees (No. 23/ USA No. 1 in 1966); **THE DAY I MET MARIE** Cliff Richard (No. 10).

6 But a more recent hit in the USA (No. 5 in 1964) stemmed from Betty Everett & Jerry Butler.

Shades Of Rock, released in 1970, provided a superabundance of chart covers, but they were not (as the Album title might suggest) just older charting classics of the genre (**LUCILLE / JOHNNY B GOODE / BONY MORONIE / WHAT'D I SAY / MEMPHIS (TENNESSEE)**), but songs of more recent vintage:
(I CAN'T GET NO) SATISFACTION The Rolling Stones (UK/USA No. 1 in 1965), **RIVER DEEP, MOUNTAIN HIGH** Ike & Tina Turner (1966 No. 3 ~ 1969 No. 33), **PAPERBACK WRITER** The Beatles (UK/USA No. 1 in 1966), **PROUD MARY** Creedance Clearwater Revival (UK No. 8/ USA No. 2 in 1969), **GET BACK** The Beatles (UK/ USA No. 1 in 1969), **SOMETHING** id. (UK No. 4/ USA No. 3 in 1969).

Rockin' With Curly Leads (1973) offered a much reduced helping of chart successes: Medley **PINBALL WIZARD** (The Who: UK No. 4/ USA No. 9 in 1969) + **SEE ME FEEL ME** (both together The New Seekers, UK No. 16/ USA No. 29 in 1973); and **GOOD VIBRATIONS** (The Beach Boys, UK/USA No. 1 in 1966).

Specs Appeal from 1975, half a "Eurovision" Album, had just **GOD ONLY KNOWS** (The Beach Boys, UK No. 2/ USA No. 39 in 1966), but[7] some of the tracks laid down at this time were carried forward on to *Tasty* (1977), an LP offering: **WALK DON'T RUN** The Ventures[8] 1960 (UK No. 8/ USA No. 2 in 1960); **HONKY TONK WOMEN** The Rolling Stones (UK/USA No. 1 in 1969); **SUPERSTAR** The Carpenters (UK No. 18/ USA No. 2 in 1971); **GOODBYE YELLOW BRICK ROAD** Elton John (UK No. 6/ USA No. 2 in 1973); **THE MOST BEAUTIFUL GIRL** Charlie Rich (UK No. 2 in 1974/ USA No. 1 in 1973).

[7] Also in 1975, the *Live At The Paris Olympia* Album worked in some early rock 'n' roll numbers.
[8] Also of course a UK chart entry by The John Barry Seven, with echoes of The Ventures but not a slavish imitation by any means.

But it is the 1979 set *String Of Hits* that brings us to the point where a really meaningful comparison can be made with certain Polydor Albums. Eleven[9] of the twelve tracks on this No. 1 Album are covers, as follows:

• From the 1960s:

RIDERS IN THE SKY The Ramrods (UK No. 8/ USA No. 30 in 1961)

CLASSICAL GAS Mason Williams (UK No. 9/ USA No. 2 in 1968/69)

• From the 1970s, the majority, some very recent:

1970:

BRIDGE OVER TROUBLED WATER Simon & Garfunkel (UK/USA No. 1), then a jump to:

1976:

RODRIGO'S GUITAR CONCERTO, popularised this year by [Geoff Love ~] Manuel & The Music Of The Mountains (No. 3); also John Williams: LP *Concerto de Aranjuez* (No. 20).

1978:

YOU'RE THE ONE THAT I WANT John Travolta & Olivia Newton-John (UK/USA No. 1)

DON'T CRY FOR ME ARGENTINA Julie Covington (UK No. 1)

BAKER STREET Gerry Rafferty (UK No. 3/ USA No. 2)

1979:

HEART OF GLASS Blondie (UK/USA No. 1)

BRIGHT EYES Art Garfunkel (UK No. 1)

PARISIENNE WALKWAYS Gary Moore (UK No. 8)

Also:

THEME FROM THE DEER HUNTER from the 1978 movie, a hit in 1979 for The Shadows (No. 9) and also for John Williams (No. 13).

****

There are a few more tracks not picked up so far:

• 1969 Album *Live At The Sankei Hall Japan*: apart from Lonnie Donegan's **PUTTING ON THE STYLE** (UK No. 1, 1957), there is **EXODUS** (Ferrante & Teicher, UK No. 6/ USA No. 2 in 1961).

• 1992 CD *More Tasty*: **THE AIR THAT I BREATHE** (The Hollies, UK No. 2/ USA No. 6 in 1974)

• 1993 CD *Everything Of Value*: **GIRL FROM IPANEMA** (Getz-Gilberto-Gilberto, UK No. 29/ USA No. 5 in 1964).

---

[9] The exception is SONG FOR DUKE (see on #2 in the main text). The originally scheduled BLACK IS BLACK, a cover of Los Lobos' hit of 1966 (UK No. 2/ USA No. 4) was put out subsequently (rather untidily) on the 1980 Album *Another String Of Hot Hits* (see *The Shadows At EMI* 370–371).

B. OTHER TRACKS

One important Singles track not so far mentioned is **SHAZAM!** (1963 B-side: Duane Eddy No. 4, 1960). Both **SOMEWHERE** (B-side 1967) and **SLAUGHTER ON TENTH AVENUE** (A-side 1969) have forerunners in the UK/USA charts, which may have been but probably were not[10] relevant to The Shadows' choice.

****

The Shadows were not averse to turning their hand to chart material in their live performances, and the above mentioned items represent the tip of the iceburg — but that is another story.

[10] For the case of SOMEWHERE, reportedly suggested by fan David Gosling to Norrie Paramor, see *Shadsfax* 25 (1999) 25.

INDEX OF TITLES

References are to the individually numbered entries in the Annual Surveys. Closely related releases are grouped together by a forward slash or slashes, so for example in the case of

CHAIN REACTION 44/58/86; 84; 87

the first three entries are related, the last two are distinct from those and from each other.

THE END OF AN ERA

The Shads' final venue: Southampton 1 December 1990
Photographs: David Hawley

SOME REVIEWERS' COMMENTS ON *THE SHADOWS AT EMI*

• "An astonishing work and ... definitely the most accurate and authoritative single volume on the subject ... a wonderful book ... indispensable and an essential purchase"

Rob Bradford *Shadsfax*

• "A meticulously well researched and presented work. Shadows fanatics can offer no reasonable excuse for not having this magnificent, indeed definitive, opus to hand"

John Campbell *Penumbra Website* (New Zealand)

• "A statistical delight for the committed Shadows aficionado ... the volume will surely satisfy even the most dedicated fact-seeker's appetite"

Russell Newmark *Record Collector*

• "A masterpiece of Shadows history in the EMI vinyl period ... an absolute must for every avid Shadows fan and collector"

Bob Gregory *ShadowMusic Website*

• "His accuracy is exemplary and his material comes from a vast range of sources. All the fans will want this, without doubt ..."

Roger Newell *Guitarist*

• "A great new book ... thoroughly recommended for all Cliff and Shadows fans"

William Hooper *Cliff Richard Website*

• "I would unhesitatingly recommend this"

Jim Nugent *Pipeline*

• "Superb ... The sheer quantity of information provided within its 464 pages is truly stunning ... a gem"

David Dixon *Shadows Website*

• "Full of useful information on the instrumental group to end them all"

Michael Heatley *Record Buyer & Music Collector*

• "Malcolm has surpassed himself ... An absolute must!"

Ulrich Sasu *Reflection* (Germany)

• " ... staggeringly good reference books ... truly absorbing ... a goldmine of facts"

Les Woosey *Shadsfax*

• "Indispensable"

Bernard Broche *Established 1958* (France)